Managing Behaviour in the Early Years

Related titles

Getting the Buggers to Behave 2 – Sue Cowley
Managing your Classroom – Gererd Dixie

Other titles in The Behaviour Management
Series

Dos and Don'ts of Behaviour Management – Roger Dunn
Managing Very Challenging Behaviour – Louisa Leaman
Managing Boys' Behaviour – Tabatha Rayment

Managing Behaviour in the Early Years

Janet Kay

continuum
NEW YORK · LONDON

Continuum International Publishing Group

The Tower Building   15 East 26th Street
11 York Road   New York, NY 10010
London SE1 7NX

www.continuumbooks.com

British Library Cataloguing-in-Publication Data
A catalogue record for this book is available from the British Library.

ISBN 0–8264–8465–4

Library of Congress Cataloging-in-Publication Data
Kay Janet.
  Managing behaviour in the early years / Janet Kay.
     p. cm.
  ISBN 0–8264–8465–4
  1. Child development. 2. Child behavior. I. Title: Managing behavior in the
early years. II. Title
HQ772.K39 2006
649'.64—dc22

                                        2005051781

Typeset by RefineCatch Limited, Bungay, Suffolk
Printed and bound in Great Britain by MPG Books Ltd, Bodmin, Cornwall

Contents

Introduction

Managing young children's behaviour is an issue that is significant for all early years practitioners in a wide range of settings. Increasing numbers of children are now attending pre-school settings and with this increase there is now more awareness of behavioural problems in the early years. In addition, there is evidence that more severe or persistent behavioural difficulties in older primary and secondary school children may well have their genesis in the early years. Studies show that early disruptions in behaviour are more strongly associated with severe and persistent behavioural problems than when these start at a later age (Moffit, 1993; Pierce, Ewing and Campbell, 1999).

Another key feature is the link between behavioural problems and learning difficulties in young children (Foot et al., 2004). Children who have learning problems may find it harder to access the curriculum, learn, develop, make friends and enjoy their early years care and education experiences. Children with learning difficulties are also more likely to develop behavioural problems. The Ofsted report *Managing Challenging Behaviour* (March 2005) found that in early years settings children with poor language and social skills and limited concentration were likely to be the children who developed behavioural problems. They also found a strong link between poor development of literacy skills and behavioural problems.

Not all behaviour management is associated with long-term issues for children. Some children may develop challenging behaviour for shorter periods of time as part of their developmental stage and progress or in response to particular stresses in their environment. Other children may be seen to have behavioural problems because there is a mismatch between behavioural expectations at home and in the setting. Managing young children's behaviour effectively is part of your contribution to their developmental progress and general well being in both the short- and long-term.

This book is aimed at early years practitioners, their managers, students and tutors on early years courses and parents interested in developing their understanding and skills in behaviour management. In the context of this book 'early years' will refer to children aged 0–8 years old in children's centres, nurseries, pre-schools, school, at home or the childminder's and any other

setting where children spend time. 'Early years practitioner' refers to anyone working in these types of
settings in any capacity and could include teachers,
teaching assistants, nursery nurses, playworkers, pre-
school workers and volunteers. 'Behaviour management'
refers to policies, strategies, activities and responses
aimed at supporting positive behaviour in young
children and reducing negative or harmful behaviour.

The book does not just focus on managing difficult or
unwanted behaviour, but also looks at long-term strategies for supporting the development of mature and
independent behaviour in children and developing their
social skills with adults and other children. Managing
behaviour is not a single issue but encompasses the
whole range of interactions between adults and children. In this book behaviour management will be discussed in the context of this range of interactions, not as
a separate event that takes place when unwanted
behaviour is encountered. Some of the reasons for difficult or unwanted behaviour will be discussed along
with the social, cultural and family factors that may
influence how a child's behaviour develops. These will
include the particular issues influencing the behaviour of
children with disabilities and learning difficulties.

The book emphasizes the role of good relationships
in behaviour management and the role of practitioners
in managing behaviour in the context of these
relationships. It includes discussion of the impact of

different behaviour management approaches on children's well-being and development and a range of strategies for managing behaviour in supportive, effective ways.

In this book you will find case studies to illustrate some of the issues raised; points for reflection or discussion; self-assessment exercises; and action points to encourage you to gather information or resources to support your skills in managing behaviour. These are intended to help you extend your understanding and to reflect on your own stage of development in this area. There is also a list of further reading at the end of the book for those who wish to continue their study in this area. Throughout the book the terms 'she' and 'he' and so on are used randomly to avoid the more clumsy s/he and him/her.

1 The Wider Policy Context for Managing Behaviour

In this chapter, the wider policy context for behaviour management is discussed in terms of changing approaches to disciplining children and the development of more child-centred views on behaviour management. Changes of attitudes to and policy around smacking are used as an example to illustrate these developments. Current approaches to behaviour management are discussed, with reference to recent policy impacting on approaches to managing behaviour in early years settings.

The Changing Context for Behaviour Management

The ways in which children's unwanted behaviour have been managed in the past vary a great deal from what is expected now. The concept of managing behaviour as opposed to punishing unwanted behaviour is relatively recent. In the past, it was not uncommon for children to be beaten, denied food, locked in small spaces and subjected to other forms of severe punishment for not conforming to adult expectations. Throughout history children have been treated with great cruelty and demeaning and harmful punishments were common-place. For the duration of most of the twentieth century physical punishment was seen as both necessary and deserved by children. In schools and at home children who misbehaved were commonly struck with imple-ments such as canes and slippers as punishments. The saying 'spare the rod and spoil the child' was considered to be a truism and parents, teachers and other authority figures considered it their role to ensure children were properly punished for 'bad' behaviour.

In more recent years the development of child-centred approaches to the education and care of young children have changed the ways in which children's behaviour is viewed and managed. These changes have been brought about by shifts in cultural norms and atti-tudes which have influenced views on children and childhood, and a greater understanding of child devel-opment which has changed our understanding of the best approaches to disciplining children. The changes have come about gradually and have been the subject of ongoing debate between professional organizations, government, practitioners, parents, researchers and theorists. Children are no longer necessarily seen as being 'bad' and needing to have naughtiness knocked out of them. Instead, helping children develop mature, socially acceptable behaviour is seen as part of their learning and development, to be promoted and supported by adults around them.

Alongside this change in how children's behaviour is seen have been changes in how their behaviour is understood. The development of psychology as a discipline has been central to a much deeper understanding of why children behave as they do and the possible causes of unwanted behaviour. In addition, there have been developments in our understanding of the impact of harsh and severe punishments on children's self-esteem and self-image in particular and this has supported a move towards milder disciplinary measures that do not undermine the child's growing sense of self or have short- or long-term negative effects on the child's development. There have also been developments in our understanding of the links between severe physical punishments and child abuse, with a number of well-known cases of child death publicized in the media to underline the extreme dangers of escalating physical punishment of children.

The Debate about Smacking

The debate about smacking children and the consequent policy changes that have taken place since the latter part of the twentieth century exemplify changing attitudes towards disciplining children and the move away from punishment to management. Attitudes towards physical punishments have changed in the last thirty years or so, with a gradual but definitive move away from more extreme methods towards milder forms. One of the fiercest debates has been about the use of smacking as a disciplinary measure. For a long time, smacking was accepted as an unremarkable form of punishment for children of all ages. Most children were smacked and this was not considered to be a cruel or unusual punishment. However, towards the end of the twentieth century a growing body of professional and voluntary organizations, parents groups and other interested agencies became involved in a long-running and heated debate about the use of smacking, which continues today despite recent legislation to limit parental use of physical punishment to mild forms.

There are a number of strands to the anti-smacking part of this debate, including:

♦ opposition to smacking on the grounds that it demeans the child;

- a demand for children to have the same right of protection from assault as adults have;

- concerns that smacking can lead to physical abuse;

- a belief that smacking contravenes children's human rights;

- a belief that smacking is ineffectual as a deterrent to future unwanted behaviour.

The pro-smacking lobby also presents a number of arguments:

- smacking is supported by some Christian organizations who believe that physical punishment is an essential component of raising children in the Christian faith;

- a belief that anti-smacking legislation is a gross intrusion into parents' rights to raise their children as they see fit;

- a belief that smacking is a desirable and effective punishment and a deterrent to future unwanted behaviour;

- a belief that failure to discipline children effectively has led to truancy, anti-social behaviour and youth crime.

The debate around smacking has mirrored changes in cultural beliefs about children and childhood. The development of child-centred approaches to parenting and the emergence of a strong children's rights lobby have changed the face of adult–child interactions in the home and in education and care settings. The ways in which adults relate to children and expect children to relate to them have changed considerably in recent years. One aspect of this change has been a gradual but persistent reduction in the incidence of physical punishment of children, initially in schools and other education and care settings and, later on, in the home. Physical punishment of children has been outlawed in state-funded schools since 1986, and in fee-paying schools since 1998. In 2005, Section 58 of the *Children Act, 2004* was implemented, banning parents from smacking children to the extent of causing 'actual bodily harm' but continuing to allow smacking that does not cause a bruise, mark or other injury.

Milestones in these developments include:

1968	Society of Teachers Opposed to Physical Punishment (STOPP) formed to campaign against all forms of corporal punishment in schools.
1979–82	Campbell and Cosan challenged the corporal punishment of their children in school

through the European Court of Human Rights and had their challenge upheld. In 1982 the ECHR ruled that beating schoolchildren against their parents' wishes must stop.

1986   Beating of children in state- and publicly-funded schools was outlawed.

1989   *United Nations Convention on the Rights of the Child* – Article 19 states that children have a right to be protected against violence.

1998   The ban on beating was extended to fee-paying schools.

1998   *Human Rights Act 1998* made it the law that any person (including children) has the right to be protected against inhuman and degrading treatment.

1998   *School Standards and Framework Act 1998* extended the ban on corporal punishment to include independent and maintained nursery schools.

1998   European Court of Human Rights ruled that the UK should clarify law on physical punishment in the home.

2003   Childminders banned from smacking.

2005   Section 58 of *Children Act, 2004* implemented in January 2005 outlawing physical punishment by parents that causes 'actual bodily harm' but allowing the continuation of 'reasonable punishment'.

| 2005 | February 2005 – the ban on corporal pun-ishment in schools challenged unsuccess-fully through the courts by a group of independent Christian schools. |

However, despite these developments, many anti-smacking groups such as Children are Unbeatable (a coalition of 300 organizations) believe that in the UK there has been a failure to fully tackle the smacking issue with an outright ban. Despite the recent legislation, mild forms of smacking are still legal in the home. In eight other European countries, smacking is completely banned at home and school (Latvia, Croatia, Sweden, Cyprus, Austria, Norway, Denmark and Finland). The campaign for a complete ban on smacking continues, as does the fierce opposition from groups such as the independent Christian schools and some parents' groups whose members wish to retain the right to smack in law.

What Sort of Behaviour is Wanted?

It is difficult in some senses to describe the types of behaviour this book refers to in terms of 'behaviour that needs managing'. While some forms of behaviour are clearly very challenging, harmful to others or disruptive to the learning processes or routines of the setting, others are more debatable. In addition, individual practitioners may have varying views of or tolerance levels for different types of children's behaviour and as such may react differently to it. Even more confusingly, behaviour in one child may to some practitioners seem more acceptable than similar behaviour in another child, depending on how regularly this behaviour is shown and whether it is in the context of generally acceptable or generally challenging behaviour patterns demonstrated by the child.

As consistency and clarity have been found to be central factors in effective behaviour management (Ofsted, March 2005), it is important that settings tackle this issue. A key factor is that early years settings need to develop a common view of what behaviour is required within the setting and this needs to be shared by all staff. The process of developing a common view is also important in developing ideas about behaviour management and how best this can be achieved as a whole-setting strategy. This is discussed further in Chapter 5.

Some of the behaviours that may be seen as a focus for positive development strategies in early years settings are:

♦ respect for others, politeness, consideration and kindness;

♦ concentration and focus on learning and other activities;

♦ demonstration of confidence and good self-esteem in learning and social development;

♦ supportive and inclusive behaviour towards all others;

♦ pro-active rather than passive responses to a range of situations;

♦ considered and well-thought-out responses to situations;

♦ calm approaches to concerns, anxieties and stressful situations.

Obviously, young children will take time to develop these behaviours and there will be many errors along the way in their understanding of what is expected and how to achieve this. Looking at this list, many adults would find it hard to claim they behave so constructively. However, it is important, if we are framing behaviour as a positive aspect of children's development, that settings put in place clear goals for behavioural development and support children in these.

Some behaviours that may be considered challenging in young children are:

- verbal challenges such as rudeness, swearing and racist or other offensive remarks to others;

- constant demanding and attention-seeking behaviour;

- repeated refusal to engage with learning activities or join in;

- aggression or physical attacks on others;

- bullying behaviour towards others;

- confrontational behaviour with adults and/or children;

- repeatedly distracting or interfering with others' play or activities;

- consistent failure to settle, concentrate or engage with activities or play;

- destructiveness e.g. learning materials or others' property;

- 'winding up' the practitioner or other children with comments, facial expressions, gestures or other persistent annoying behaviour;

- consistent failure to comply with requests or follow routines;

- patterns of behaviour that contain several of the elements above and that are repeated and persistent and do not respond to intervention from the practitioner/early years setting.

Words like 'consistent' and 'repeated' and 'constant' appear here because many behaviours that would not be considered problematical if they were occasional are considered challenging if they are persistent or part of a pattern of behaviour. It is important to remember that this list is not definitive but indicative of some of the behaviours that practitioners and early years settings may view as challenging in young children.

Current Thinking about Behaviour Management

As discussed above, there have been changes in our understanding of and responses to young children's behaviour in more recent times. Behaviourist approaches have dominated behaviour management in education and other disciplines, including parenting support, for many years. Weare (2004: 62) argues that many schools still 'tackle what they see as "bad" behaviour by the age-old responses of identification, punishment, containment and exclusion' despite the fact that there is little evidence to support this approach.

However, simple concepts of reward and punishment

are being challenged by more demanding ideas about how children's behaviour should be responded to in the context of their holistic developmental needs. Within this latter approach, behaviour is seen as an aspect of development, to be responded to, nurtured and promoted as with any other aspect.

As such, it is now recognized that behaviour management needs to be considered within a range of strategies to facilitate the promotion of all aspects of a child's development, not just in terms of bringing about changes in behaviour. For example, harsher punishments may bring about such changes in behaviour, but this may be at the expense of other aspects of a child's developmental progress. In one case, a child who was told off in sharp, critical tones for taking a long time to go the toilet during a session was humiliated in front of other children and made to feel conspicuous. She did not contribute during the rest of the session, but sat with her head down trying to hide flushed pink cheeks. The approach used had left her embarrassed and self-conscious. Weare (2004) suggests that punishment does not work with children who may have reasons not to fit in easily with the behavioural demands of the setting because of their social and cultural background, emotional state or difficulties with learning. More recent behaviour management strategies emphasize that best practice focuses on supporting and developing children's positive behaviour in the context of meeting all their developmental needs. Weare (2004) argues that behaviour management should take place as part of the development of emotionally literate schools, which involves centralizing support for children's emotional and social competence.

Teaching children acceptable behaviour is part of the early years practitioner's role, and as such, it is recognized that this is a developmental process that takes place over time. It is also recognized that young children will present with very different kinds of behaviour depending on their unique personal circumstances: their developmental stage; their personality and characteristics; and their social and cultural background (as discussed in Chapter 2).

In this context, behaviour management is a more complex concept. In the past, when behavioural norms were rigidly determined by adults and enforced by power-assertion techniques such as corporal punishment, it was simpler for adults operating behaviour management systems. Children were seen more often as 'good' or 'naughty' and behaviour was seen as 'good' or 'bad'. More recent approaches to behaviour management recognize that these polarized concepts are based on value-judgements and that within this type of approach the quality of children's behaviour is determined subjectively, with only a limited range of adult-determined behaviours seen as acceptable. So, for one adult, a child who asks a lot of questions may be seen as keen, inquisitive, eager to learn and interested in the topic. Another adult may determine a stream of questions as intrusive, disruptive, unnecessary, threatening the stability of the session and promoting unwanted debate among others.

Behaviour management strategies that strongly promote conformity may also ignore the fact that their developmental stage, family and cultural backgrounds and early experiences are some of the determinants of children's behaviour. When children enter care and education settings they come with a huge range of different experiences. Part of this experience will be their unique understandings of behavioural norms and expectations. For one child, certain behaviours may have been perfectly acceptable in their home and community; for another child there may have been a different response to the same types of behaviour. Children need time to learn what is expected of them and the maturity to recognize that expectations may be different in different contexts. Learning about expectations and behavioural requirements may be easier or harder for a child depending on the correlation between the requirements of the home and the setting. Parenting styles and child-rearing practices differ between families meaning that children may present a whole range of different behaviours, all of which have been acceptable within their homes, but some of which may be less acceptable in the setting. It is important that settings accept these differences and, without compromising behavioural standards, accommodate diversity in this area. Home and environmental influences are discussed more fully in Chapter 2.

Despite the trend against severe punishments, approaches to behaviour management that depend on reward and punishment are, however, still very common. Porter (2003) contrasts two approaches, describing them as 'controlling' and 'guidance' styles of managing behaviour, and argues that guidance methods are more effective because they focus on developing the child's considerateness, whilst controlling methods have a number of flaws.

These include:

♦ the approach is based on training children to comply with adult directives rather than learning self-determination, self-control and cooperative skills;

♦ it encompasses a negative view of children and assumes that without controlling systems they will behave 'badly';

♦ it may result in deteriorations in behaviour as children respond negatively to punishments;

♦ controlling methods are less effective than guidance methods, particularly with children who need behavioural change but are already not responding to rewards and punishments;

♦ controlling methods may have a detrimental effect on children's self-esteem.

Porter also argues that rewards and punishments are in opposition to the developmental approaches generally accepted as the best methods of supporting children's learning and other aspects of development. While it is accepted that children will make errors in some areas of their development, these are not tolerated in terms of their behavioural development. While it is also accepted that children are motivated to progress and make steps forward of their own volition in terms of their learning and other aspects of development, it is assumed that they will not do this without a rewards and punishment approach in terms of their behaviour.

Porter concludes:

> In contrast, a guidance approach accepts that behavioural mistakes are as inevitable as develop-mental errors and so, rather than punishing chil-dren for these, will teach them how to acquire more skills. Given the inevitability of errors during childhood, if we were to punish children for making mistakes, we would be punishing them for being children.
>
> (2003: 18)

To summarize, the behaviour management strategies discussed in this book are based on:

Managing Behaviour in the Early Years

♦ The belief that behaviour must be managed within the context of children's holistic development so that behaviour management does not have a negative effect on other aspects of development.

♦ A recognition that children's behaviour varies considerably in response to different cultural, parenting and other early experiences.

♦ The belief that children's behaviour changes over time like any other aspect of their development and that behaviour management involves teaching children behavioural skills to support progress.

♦ A recognition that many influences within and outside the setting will shape a child's unique development and their behavioural development will be a product of this process.

♦ The belief that children's behaviour has meaning and that simple behaviouristic responses may not be effective as they fail to acknowledge or take into account that meaning.

The Current Policy Context

Every major policy document currently influencing practice in the early years emphasizes the need to develop warm, nurturing, respectful relationships with children and to use mild and non-demeaning forms of discipline that support children's development and which do not damage their self-esteem. However, it is also clear that current policy emphasizes the role of good-quality teaching and learning in well-organized and structured environments to give children a sense of security and purpose.

The Elton Report (DES, 1989) had a significant impact on ideas and developments in managing behaviour in schools, mainly through its focus on positive, rather than reactive, approaches to behaviour management. The Committee of Enquiry was set up to investigate concerns about lack of discipline in schools and fears of increased aggression towards teachers. The report firmly placed the role of good-quality teaching and learning at the heart of behaviour management by stating that 80 per cent of disruption in schools is 'directly attributable to poor classroom organization, planning and teaching'. It recommended that behaviour management should be promoted in a positive and planned way and promoted whole-school approaches to developing good behavioural standards. Key issues were the links between behaviour and curriculum content and delivery and the general organization of the teaching and learning in the classroom and school. The report recommended that:

- schools should have a clear vision of how they will manage behaviour;

- that policies should emphasize positive behaviour rather than discipline;

- teachers should be role models;

- good behaviour should be rewarded.

The Elton Report gave guidance on policies and codes of conduct, advising that positive behaviour should be encouraged and that it should be made clear to children what types of behaviour were considered positive or unwanted. Hanko (2003) argues that the Elton Report promoted collaborative, problem-solving approaches to behaviour management with the development of insight into the needs of children with emotional and behavioural difficulties within curriculum planning.

The *Curriculum Guidance for the Foundation Stage* (QCA, 2000) sets out principles for good practice in working with children aged 3–5 years that are relevant to developing positive behaviour. They emphasize the skills of practitioners in relating to children and developing an effective curriculum that is carefully structured and builds on what children already know. They also emphasize that practitioners need to know about child development and have the ability to observe and respond to children's needs. The guidance also focuses on inclusion and working in partnership with parents as key aspects of good practice. Perhaps the most significant guidance relates to meeting diverse needs, which promotes inclusion and the ability of practitioners and settings to promote and support the needs of all children. The guidance states:

> Practitioners must be aware that children bring to their early learning provision different experiences, interests, skills and knowledge that affect their ability to learn.
>
> (QCA, 2000: 17)

The guidance effectively emphasizes aspects of practice that are relevant to the promotion of a well-managed environment in which behaviour management takes place in the context of good early years practice and support for all children's needs. This is also emphasized when discussing the management of behaviour in respect of children with SEN and disabilities.

The role of early years settings in supporting the development of positive behaviour is one theme of Sylva et al.'s *The Effective Provision of Pre-School Education (EPPE) Project* (EPPE, 2003). The study focused on many aspects of early years provision to determine its value to young children's holistic development. They concluded that 'EPPE has demonstrated the positive effects of high quality provision on children's intellectual and social/

behavioural development' (EPPE, 2003: 1). They found that high-quality pre-school settings characterized by well-qualified staff; warm and responsive relationships between staff and children; a balance between child- and adult-directed activities; and high standards of content and in the delivery of the curriculum, had a direct positive impact on reducing anti-social/worried behaviour in young children.

The Ofsted publication *Managing Challenging Behaviour* (March 2005) reports on behaviour management in early years centres, primary and secondary schools and colleges. It concludes that, while the majority of children and young people behave well in educational settings, there remains a number (usually small in each setting) of children whose disruptive behaviour is a problem. In line with current thinking, the report recommends that children are best supported by:

♦ respectful behaviour from teachers and other staff;

♦ organized classrooms and well-maintained environments;

♦ clearly established routines;

♦ a cheerful greeting at the start of the day;

♦ strategies to engage the children and hold their interest;

♦ consistent and non-confrontational behaviour from the teacher.

Other significant issues are the relationships that settings have with parents and other agencies. Early years centres and primary schools were found to have generally good relationships with parents, often in early years centres involving daily contact and a clear common understanding of the child's needs and how these would be met. However, the relationship between LEAs and early years centres was found to be generally poor, and the relationship with other agencies, particularly social services, was found to be generally poor for all educational settings.

It is clear that managing behaviour in the current policy context is not mainly about devising disciplinary measures, but focuses on developing a whole-setting philosophy and approach that develops a nurturing and creative environment in which all aspects of all children's development is promoted. This focus places a great deal of responsibility on individual practitioners and settings to develop effective behaviour management policies and practices. However, staff may not always be fully equipped to do this. For example, the *Standards for the Award of Qualified Teacher Status* (DfES/TTA, 2002) now have an increased emphasis on training in behaviour management, with trainees having to demonstrate that:

♦ they know a range of strategies to promote good behaviour and establish a purposeful learning environment;

♦ they set high expectations for pupils' behaviour and establish a clear framework for classroom discipline to anticipate and manage pupils' behaviour constructively, and promote self-control and independence.

In fact, however, trainees often report that they have not had sufficient guidance in their training to manage behaviour effectively and that they do not have sufficient knowledge of child development (Ofsted, March 2005).

Policy and Inclusion

It is hard to believe in the current policy climate of inclusion that only 30 years ago in the UK, children with disabilities and learning difficulties frequently spent their lives in institutions, often hospitals, rather than in their own homes. Education was denied to many of these children and those who did receive education were isolated in special schools. Medical models of disability dominated policy and children with disabilities were seen as having medical problems that required treatment, rather than in terms of the social and functional models that currently determine thinking about disability. Cultural and social change led to this change in thinking, and new ways of supporting children with disabilities to meet their maximum developmental potential emerged in the 1980s. Disability awareness and changes in social attitudes towards disabled people became apparent alongside legislative change to include disabled children in social and educational provision for all children.

The *Children Act, 1989* identified children with disabilities as 'children in need' with entitlement to service provision for the child and family to support the child's holistic development. The *Special Educational Needs Code of Practice* (1994; 2001) provided a framework for working with children with special needs in schools and providing them with education relevant to their needs. This *Code of Practice* was revised in 2001 in accordance with the provisions of the *Special Educational Needs and Disability Act, 2001* which extended requirements for inclusive practice to all early years settings and provision. These requirements effectively mean that, as far as is possible, settings have to adapt their environments and practices, their curriculum and their attitudes in order to provide an appropriate education for children with SEN. Inclusion is supported within the legislation as follows:

- LEAs must make every effort to place children with SEN in mainstream settings;

- settings have to inform parents of any special educational provision they provide for the child;

- settings and/or parents can request a statutory assessment for SEN;

- LEAs have to provide parent partnership services to support parents of children with SEN and conflict resolution systems for resolving disagreements between parents, the LEA and the school;

- children with disability must not be discriminated against, treated less fairly than other children or disadvantaged within the setting.

Inclusion has had a significant impact on behaviour management in the early years. Initially, not all settings had the experience, training or knowledge to deal with some of the behaviours children with developmental issues brought into the setting. Inclusion has highlighted the need for effective policies and behaviour management strategies in early years settings. Children with developmental issues and behaviour are discussed further in Chapter 3 and developing inclusive settings is discussed in Chapter 5.

Summary and Conclusions

In this chapter, the development of behaviour management over time has been considered, emphasizing the
move towards developmental approaches and away
from adult-centred disciplinary approaches involving
harsher punishments, and behaviouristic approaches
focusing on rewards and punishments. Some ideas and
current thinking about the most effective approaches to
behaviour management have been considered, including the developmental guidance approach advocated
by Porter (2003) and the development of emotionally
literate schools approach (Weare, 2004). Current policy
trends have also been considered, with reference to the
role of the setting in promoting positive behaviour
through the curriculum and the impact of inclusion
policies on early years settings. However, some of the
limitations were considered with reference to Ofsted's
findings in their report *Managing Challenging Behaviour*
(March 2005).

Key features of effective behaviour management can
be summarized as follows:

♦ the development of warm, respectful and responsive
relationships between adults and children within the
setting;

♦ clear strategies for managing behaviour focused on

promoting good standards and positive attitudes, rather than disciplinary measures;

♦ a recognition that behaviour management strategies should be developed within the framework of responses to all children's holistic developmental needs;

♦ a curriculum that reflects children's needs and learning abilities and that is well-organized, engaging and relevant;

♦ good well-organized routines and a well-managed setting;

♦ well-trained staff who are good role models for children and who have a range of skills to respond effectively to children's behavioural needs;

♦ good levels of communication and partnership with parents and other relevant professionals and/or agencies.

2 Environmental Influences on Children's Development and Behaviour

In this chapter, the discussion focuses on the range of influences on young children's behaviour. Current views on how behaviour is conceptualized in the context of environmental influences on young children's overall development are discussed in order to develop better understanding of the complex factors that shape children's behaviour. Knowledge and understanding of these factors are crucial to every practitioner's ability to develop appropriate responses to individual children's behaviour and to work with parents and other professionals towards helping individual and groups of children to develop their behaviour appropriately.

The impact of disabilities and learning difficulties on behaviour is discussed in Chapter 3.

Ecological Approaches to Understanding Behaviour

Managing behaviour takes place in the context of both the setting and the child's developmental stage at the time. However, young children's behaviour within early years settings is not just influenced by the events of the moment or within the context of the setting. Young children's behaviour is usually based on patterns, events and expectations developed outside the setting, as well as those developed within the setting. As any early years practitioner knows, the causes of the behaviour you deal with in the setting often have their roots in relationships and events in the home or the wider context in which the child lives. Effectively, young children's behaviour has meaning for them in the context of their own experiences, and understanding this meaning is central to effectively supporting children's behavioural development.

Annie and Joe (6 years old)

Understanding the complex influences on young children's behaviour can be crucial in determining effective responses to support the child and to improve the behaviour. These two case studies highlight the different influences on young children and the outcomes of these for their behaviour.

Annie

Annie got up at 7.45am after sleeping for 12 hours. She had a bath and a story before bed and both her parents kissed her good night and tucked her in. This morning, Annie had cereal and fruit juice for breakfast and a small piece of toast. She had a chat with her mum about dance class that night and a joke with her dad about his hair sticking up in the mornings. Her father walked her to school before going to work, saw her into the class-room and said Hello to her teacher. During first lesson, when Annie was talking while the teacher gave instruc-tions, she was asked to stop. She smiled brightly and apologized to the teacher, then paid attention carefully.

Joe

Joe went to bed at 11.30pm because he stayed up to watch a film with his older sister who was looking after him as his mother was out. He overslept this morning and didn't have time for breakfast. His mum shouted at him for being late when she had to get to work and then there was a row between his mum and his older sister about money. Joe walked to school on his own as his mum was late for work. The teacher told him twice in the first session that he needed to pay attention and when he asked Joe a question, Joe could not answer it. Joe got into a fight with another child at first break and said some very rude things to the teacher who intervened.

Managing Behaviour in the Early Years

In order to understand the causes of young children's behaviour it is increasingly understood that more needs to be known about their background and early experiences, current events in their lives outside the setting, and their relationships. Understanding the experiences that shape a child's behaviour in the setting is the basis for developing effective behaviour management strategies.

One way of looking at children's behaviour is by using ecological models, such as Bronfenbrenner's ecosystems approach (1979), which demonstrates the complex links between the different influences on the child's behaviour and development. Bronfenbrenner applied systems approaches to the study of human behaviour, developing a model that can be used to explore how children's development is shaped. This model emphasizes not only the range of influences on a child's development but also the interrelationships between the different factors. Foot et al. (2004: 116), citing Athey (1990), Banathy (1973) and Bronfenbrenner (1979), state that:

> A systems approach acknowledges the complex interrelationships between the child, significant adults and the community within which the child is located.

Ecological perspectives are increasingly influencing our understanding of children's development by demonstrating that such development is a product of the child's environment as well as the child's unique personal characteristics. As such, it is now widely recognized that young children's development is largely a product of the interactions between the child and his environment. Ecological perspectives suggest that a wide range of complex and interrelated factors in her environment influences the child's development. The child's inter-actions with these factors shape her developmental process in a way that is unique to her alone.

The child's behaviour will be influenced by these fac-tors, which may include:

♦ family type and composition;

♦ the family's social and cultural background;

♦ home setting and environment;

♦ parenting styles and child-rearing practices;

♦ relationship with parents, siblings and other family members;

♦ the family's employment and financial situation;

♦ support for learning and other aspects of develop-ment in the home;

♦ the child's own emotional needs and the extent to which these are met;

♦ the child's social skills and ability to relate to peers and adults;

♦ any disabilities which may influence the child's developmental progress;

♦ factors influencing family behaviour e.g. illness, loss of jobs, bereavement, separation and divorce.

Fig. 2.1 is an example of an ecological model showing the types of influences on a child's behaviour and how a systems approach demonstrates the links between these. The model shows how the different systems work together and interlink. The different systems are discussed in more detail below.

Microsystems:
These include the most immediate influences on the child such as home context and individual relationships within this and the child's early years setting. Each microsystem can be described separately but it is the links between these which are significant.

Mesosystems:
A mesosystem is the links and connections between the microsystems that directly affect the child. So, for example, it could relate to the quality of the relationship between the child's parents and his early years setting. The links between the systems are also significant in

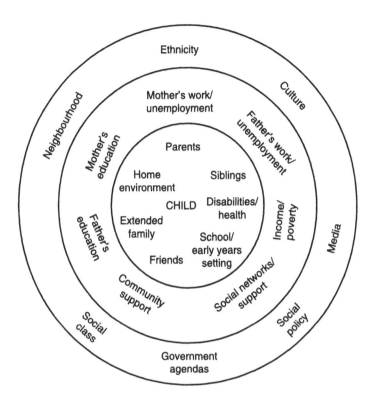

Key:–

1. *Centre* – microsystems (factors that effect the child directly) and mesosystems (the links between the microsystems, e.g. the parents' relationship with siblings)
2. *Inner circle* – exosystems (factors that indirectly affect the child by influencing one of the microsystems, e.g. the impact of job loss on a parent)
3. *Outer circle* – macrosystems (wider cultural and social setting)

Figure 2.1 Diagram of Ecological Model of Child Development

terms of how the impact of one microsystem on the child's behaviour is felt in another microsystem. The example of Joe given above helps to illustrate this. Joe's tiredness, stress and anger are generated in the home but appear in his behaviour at school. Significantly, intervention in one microsystem will affect behaviour in another (Foot et al., 2004). This has particular importance in relation to our understanding of the connections between different aspects of a child's life and how these can work together to resolve behavioural issues. For example, it has significance for practitioners and parents working together when behaviour is an issue. Returning to the example of Joe, it is clear that changes at home which ensure better sleep and nutrition for Joe and a less stressful start to the day may have a positive impact on his behaviour at school. However, the interactions between two microsystems such as school and home may not be so simple. Often the connections are circular rather than linear with influences between the different factors going both ways. So, in our example, Joe's mother may need support and advice from school in order to create the conditions at home that could help his behaviour improve. This type of circular influence is demonstrated in Fig. 2.2.

Exosystems:
These are the influences on the family such as work and employment or unemployment, social situation and

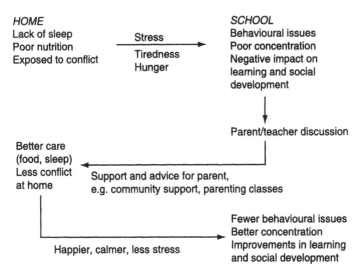

Figure 2.2 Illustration of Circular Influences Between Microsystems

the presence or absence of supportive social networks, money and income and other influences that may affect the quality of family functioning and parenting. So, for example, a child's parents could have supportive social systems including extended family. Or they could have few support networks, demanding and unsupportive extended family and no one to turn to in a crisis. Employment could be a positive influence on family functioning and parenting or long hours, poor pay and boredom could be a more negative influence.

Managing Behaviour in the Early Years

Macrosystems:
These relate to the wider culture within which the child and family are placed. This may include the community in which they live and whether this is a positive or more hostile environment, the economic and social situation of the society in which they live and the ways in which the family may relate to these. It could be exemplified by the extent to which the family feels socially excluded or included or the position and sense of acceptance of immigrant or asylum-seeking families. The way that the wider culture is influenced by social policy is also relevant, for example, in relation to economic and family policy which may influence the numbers of children and families living in poverty or not (Bee, 2000).

Ecological models demonstrate the different influences on a child that may affect aspects of development, including behaviour. However, they try to show something beyond simple causal links between these factors and the developmental outcomes for the child. The ways in which environmental factors may interact will have a significant impact on the child. For example, if a child's father leaves the home after a separation, the impact may be due to the loss of contact with the parent, but it may also be due to loss of income in the family, changes in the mother's state of mind, the reactions of siblings, and possibly a change of home and school and the loss of friends. It is the combination of these factors that will affect the child, as they interact to impact on social and emotional development, confidence and the level of support the child gets from parents.

Self-Assessment Point

Look at the case studies of Annie and Joe on page 35. With reference to Fig. 2.1, draw a model of the factors in their lives that may be affecting their behaviour and try to make links between these.

Ecological approaches can help us understand the complex influences on a child's behaviour. However, each child is unique and we cannot assume that the outcomes will be the same for children in similar situations. The child's responses to her unique experiences will depend on her existing stage of development, skills and abilities. It will also depend on her personal characteristics and the ways that these interact with the environment. For example, a child with a resilient and positive outlook may cope with stressful events better than another child who does not have these qualities to the same extent. The child is not passive in her own development but contributes to the quality of her own experiences. It is the interaction between the child and her environment that shapes her developmental progress and each child brings her own unique characteristics to this process.

Sue and Gina

Sue, 5, and Gina, 6, have just been placed with foster carers in a city suburb after their previous foster carer became too ill to care for them. They started their new school three weeks ago. Gina seems to be settling well and has already made friends in her class and progress with her work. She was a bit shy at first but is now able to ask questions and ask for help when she needs it. Although Gina is behind other children in terms of literacy development and maths in particular, her teacher feels fairly confident that she will soon start to catch up as she concentrates well and is an enthusiastic pupil who puts a lot into her work. Gina seems to understand the reasons for the move and keeps in touch with her previous foster carer by phone.

Sue has mild learning difficulties and is very shy and lacking in confidence. She has not settled at all well in her class and cries at length when she is left every morning. Sue has not made any friends and avoids making contact or joining in with other children, although many have tried to be friendly with her. The teacher is concerned that she does not speak even when spoken to, and that she is very reluctant to tackle any tasks. According to the carers, Sue has had nightmares and has started to wet the bed since the move, and she gets very upset if anyone tries to discuss her previous foster carer with her. Sue does not talk to her previous carer on the phone and the new carers are finding it difficult to help her settle in their home. The carers have told Sue's teacher that they are puzzled by this reaction as Sue was less close to the previous foster carer and Gina was the preferred child in the foster home.

Discussion Point

1. Are there any reasons you can think of for the different responses of the two children to the same situation?
2. What could the teacher do to support Sue?

Ecological approaches help us to understand the influences on children's behavioural development, and the ways in which they interact with each other and the child's unique characteristics to create particular patterns of behaviour. In the next sections, some of the environmental factors affecting children's development will be discussed in more detail. However, firstly, the impact of parental behaviour, in terms of parenting style, on the child's development and behaviour will be discussed.

Parenting Styles and Approaches

There are a number of different models of parenting styles and approaches which have been formulated through the research of theorists such as Baumrind (1967; 1973) and Maccoby and Martin (1983). These models reflect stereotypes of parenting approaches but help us understand the different experiences children have in their earliest relationships and the impact of these experiences on the child's development. A range of studies demonstrate that, while there are no direct causal links between parenting approach and children's development, the consistent use of certain parenting styles is associated with more positive or negative outcomes for children.

The impact of parenting on the child's experience is significant in terms of the child's ability to cope with the demands of the early years setting and the extent to which the child is able to access the curriculum. Poor-quality parenting can have a negative influence on aspects of development, resulting in an increased likelihood of behavioural problems arising. However, parenting approaches are not developed in a vacuum. The parent's character, the child's character and the environment in which parenting takes place are determinants of a particular parent–child relationship. This is discussed in more detail later.

Maccoby and Martin (1983) developed a four-fold model of parenting style drawing on Baumrind's original model developed through her research into parenting styles and behaviours. The types of parenting behaviours that are significant are:

♦ warmth (responsiveness, sensitivity, affection);

- communication (conversation, listening);

- control (boundaries, disciplinary measures);

- expectations (independence, behaviour, maturity).

The four types of parenting Maccoby and Martin identified have strongly influenced our understanding of the link between parenting and developmental outcomes for the child.

1. Permissive Parenting

Permissive parents are generally loving and communicative with their children and can be responsive and sensitive to their needs. However, they tend to be less likely to set clear boundaries or expectations around behaviour and their expectations of the child in terms of behaviour and achievement may be low. Typically, the child may be nurtured but may not develop consideration for others and the ability to behave independently. Without clear boundaries and guidance, the child may be insecure and unhappy. The child's behaviour may be egotistical and the child may behave in ways that are unacceptable to peers and adults because they fail to take into account the rights and feelings of others.

> **Shiraz**
>
> Shiraz is 3 years old. His parents have always strongly advocated freedom of expression for children and are loving and indulgent towards Shiraz. He usually gets what he wants immediately and his demands are central to the household functioning. Shiraz has major tantrums and does not manage some situations. Recently his mother had to leave a café after other customers complained because Shiraz was rampaging around the tables, shouting and throwing napkins around. Shiraz's mother is exhausted but unclear as to how to improve the situation. She has difficulty being consistent with him and tends to give in for a 'quiet life'.

2. Authoritative Parenting

Typically, authoritative parents are loving and responsive towards their children, showing warmth and sensitivity to their needs and establishing good patterns of communication early on. They have high expectations of the child's behaviour and achievements, which develop as the child matures, and they are supportive to the child's goals and ambitions. Clear boundaries are discussed, negotiated and enforced, but punishments are not severe and these parents tend to avoid power-assertion techniques such as shouting and smacking. The child of authoritative parents tends to be more mature, do better in education and be socially confident. They also tend to be more compliant with parental demands and to have fewer behavioural issues. The child tends to behave well, be compliant with adult requests and considerate of others.

Tansy

Tansy is 4. She is the middle child in a family of three children. Tansy lives with her mother and sees her father at weekends. Both parents are keen to ensure that they provide their children with consistent parenting and they discuss issues and problems regularly. Tansy is expected to behave well in general, to discuss any problems she may have and to be thoughtful of others, in line with her age and stage of development. Both parents use conversation to share ideas and plans with Tansy and to help her problem-solve. Boundaries are made clear through discussion and negotiation, and these boundaries change over time so Tansy can develop more independence. Tansy is a happy, contented child who has good relationships with parents and siblings and is getting on very well at nursery, making friends and enjoying learning.

---

3. *Authoritarian Parenting*

Authoritarian parents have high expectations of their children and may make a lot of demands of them. Boundaries are clear and well defined, but more likely to be set by the parents rather than negotiated. Conforming to parental expectations and obedience is valued but communication, flexibility and negotiation are not. Punishments may be more frequent and more severe with a higher likelihood of harsher methods being used. Responsiveness and warmth are at low levels and the changing needs of children are less understood or taken into account. Parenting is adult focused and children are expected to comply with parents' demands without consultation. Children of this type of parent tend to be either more passive or may become defiant and aggressive. They are more likely to have social problems and do less well in education.

Sanjay

Sanjay is 5. His parents have very strict views about how children should be raised and they believe that children should be unquestioningly obedient and well behaved. They do not tolerate any defiance and they strongly discourage discussion or negotiation about rules. Sanjay is punished by being sent to his room or given a smack on the hand if he is disobedient. He is expected to do well in

---

school and his father is critical of what he sees as San-jay's slow progress in reading and writing although the teacher has explained that this is perfectly normal and that Sanjay is doing fine. Sanjay's father believes boys need to be tough and 'manly' and he criticizes Sanjay's mother if she cuddles or displays affection for him. Sanjay has been in a few confrontations with other children at school where he has become angry and aggressive. Initially quite popular in nursery, other children are now starting to avoid him.

4. Neglectful Parenting

Neglectful parents tend to be low on warmth and responsiveness to their children and insensitive to their needs. They do not provide consistent boundaries or expectations and may seem to be indifferent to their children's views, opinions, progress and achievement. At the extreme end of neglectful parenting, children may not be provided with requirements of their basic physiological needs, such as adequate food and drink, warmth and care, or with sufficient emotional nurturing to develop successfully. Neglectful parents are adult centred, unlikely to understand and/or respond to the changing developmental needs of their children. Discipline and punishments may be inconsistent and arbitrary. Neglected children tend to be insecure, do less well socially and educationally and have emotional and behavioural difficulties.

Maisie

Maisie is 5. She has lived with her maternal grandmother since her parents' marriage broke up when she was 9 months old. Maisie's mother has a serious drug habit and is unable and unwilling to care for her. She rarely sees her. Maisie's father remarried and had another child shortly afterwards. He and his wife now have a second baby. Maisie's grandmother is deeply resentful about 'getting dumped' with Maisie and is constantly at loggerheads with both parents about their lack of financial contribution to her care. Maisie's father says he cannot afford to pay anything as he is looking after his other children and his new wife would not like it if money went elsewhere. Maisie's grandmother does not buy her things like clothes and toys and she is poorly fed, often going without meals. Her grandmother says there is no money for her upkeep so she will have to go without. She largely ignores Maisie, leaving her for long periods and ignoring her when she is around. Maisie is poorly dressed, thin and unkempt. She does not speak much at school and has not made any friends. She was often absent from nursery but now walks herself to school, arriving early. Maisie often refuses to tackle new tasks, cries easily and becomes upset if asked questions.

The Impact of Parenting on the Child's Behaviour

Parenting styles are not the only determinants of children's behaviour, but they create the context in which the child's development takes place and this may influence how the child responds to different situations and events and the resources and skills the child has to deal with these. There is evidence that children who are disruptive in early years and other educational settings often have disadvantages and disturbances in their family lives (Ofsted, March 2005). Many have special educational needs and for some children this, again, can be linked to poor developmental experiences in the early years. This is particularly significant for children who are in public care who may have had disruptions in their care and poor attachments to carers. For many children in public care, early experiences have been limited or poor and parenting has been of a low quality with a high proportion suffering abuse and/or neglect.

Although incidence of behavioural problems increases with the child's age, 20 per cent of behavioural problems in primary schools are associated with children aged 4–6 years old. There is a link between young children starting school without the social and emotional skills to cope, and the development of behavioural issues, particularly disruptive behaviour. In the discussion on parenting styles, it is clear that the quality of the parenting approach is firmly linked to the child's positive social and emotional development.

Authoritative parenting styles are considered to provide the child with the most consistently positive context for developing successfully in terms of mature behaviour, good social skills, emotional stability and self-control, and effective learning skills. No parent will parent consistently all the time and most parents use a range of parenting styles over time and in different situations. As the child grows and changes, parenting styles may also change in response to the child's different needs.

Children may find it difficult to respond to very different approaches to behaviour management between the early years setting and home and they may behave in ways that are shaped by their parenting experiences. As such, behaviour that may be considered unacceptable in the setting may be acceptable at home or vice versa. Children who are insecure and anxious in their home environments may act this out through demanding, difficult behaviour in the setting.

The Determinants of Parenting Style

The determinants of a parent's approach to parenting are complex. Belsky's (1984) model of the influences on

parenting demonstrates how these determinants interact to create a parent's individual approach to childcare.
Fig. 2.3 gives an example of the interrelated factors
influencing a mother's parental functioning.

The parent's own experiences of parenting, their own
developmental experiences and the extent of their social
and emotional support systems are crucial factors in
determining their approach to caring for their own children. However, many other factors can influence parenting style and these may affect parenting at different

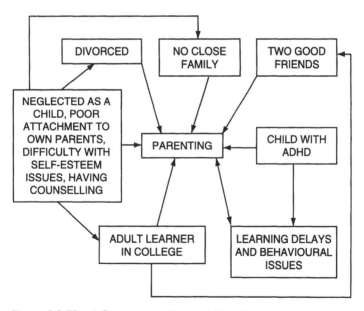

Figure 2.3 The Influences on Parental Functioning – an example
(from Belsky, 1984)

times. For example, there is evidence that during and after divorce, parenting may become more authoritarian. Parents who are depressed may be less responsive, more irritable and resentful of their children. However, it is also important to remember that parenting will also be shaped by the child's characteristics and behaviour and that many parents use different approaches with their different children depending on this. The relationship between the child and parent is not one directional but influenced by both. Belsky and Vondra (1989: 170) state:

> It is now widely recognised that what transpires in the parent–child relationship is determined not only by the parent, but by the child as well . . . . we speak, therefore, in terms of bi-directional influences.
>
> (in Ghate and Hazel, 2002: 45)

Poverty

One of the major influences on children's overall development is the extent to which they live in poverty. In the UK at present, 28 per cent of children in Britain still live in poverty (3.6 million children) despite improvements since 1998 when it was one in three children, as compared to one in ten in 1979 (*End Child Poverty*, 2005).

Poverty is not just significant in terms of the child's lack of financial resources, but in terms of the impact it has on all aspects of the child's life and development. The case study below illustrates some of the factors associated with poverty that put the child at risk developmentally.

Candy

Candy is 7. She lives with her parents and two younger sisters in a run-down house on an old estate. The estate has few amenities for children or adults and there have been quite a few problems with gangs of drug dealers. Candy is not allowed to play out beyond her small garden, as her mother does not think it is safe. The family do not like where they live but cannot see any alternatives at present. They do not socialize with neighbours and Candy is not encouraged to invite other children home as her parents have had some problems with racist abuse on the largely white estate.

Candy's father has no employment at present. Her mother works shifts in a supermarket and is often out or tired from work. There are a lot of rows about money and the fact that Candy's father has been drinking more recently. He seems tired and apathetic and has little to do with the children apart from being in the house all the time. Candy's mother has been trying to get him to go to the doctor as he has no energy and sits staring at the TV all the time. She often has little energy after work and cannot often find the time to read or play games with Candy or her sisters. The family do not go on trips

---

or holidays and there are few treats, new clothes or new things for the house, which is dingy and poorly furnished.

Discussion Points

1. What is potential impact of poverty on Candy's development?
2. What sort of behavioural issues may result?

Poverty is often very stressful for both children and adults. Poor environments have been shown to have an impact on adults' ability to parent effectively. Children who live in poverty are more likely to experience neglect as parents try to fulfil their own needs or struggle to cope with lack of resources. Parents are more likely to have poor health and to use drugs or alcohol to cope. There may also be poorer relationships between parents, and there may be a lack of social support for some families, as poorer areas tend to have fewer amenities.

Ghate and Hazel (2002) explored factors that influenced parenting in poor environments and concluded in three categories of stress factors that put parenting at risk. These are:

Individual Stress Factors

♦ parents in poor environments are significantly more

likely to have poor mental, emotional and physical health problems;

♦ children in poor environments are slightly more likely to have health and behaviour problems.

Family Stress Factors:

♦ low incomes, high anxiety about money and financial problems;

♦ 40 per cent of parents had 'serious' deficiencies with their housing (p. 82);

♦ chronic lone parenthood, linked to mental health issues, particularly depression;

♦ evidence of poor-quality relationships with partners in two parent families;

♦ 30 per cent of parents had multiple stressors with three or more significant problems reported.

Community/Neighbourhood Stress Factors:

♦ environmental problems such as dog-fouling, traffic, loose dogs, pollution and litter which created anxiety about children's safety and health;

♦ crime affected 29 per cent of parents and drugs 18 per cent;

♦ freedom of movement for adults and children is curtailed by perceived dangers such as unruly behaviour, drugs and prostitution.

Not all children who are poor live in areas of disadvantage. Some children may feel they stand out in early years settings where there is a mix of socio-economic backgrounds. They may be the one who has not been to see the latest film or got the latest toy or been away on holiday or day trips in the summer. Poverty can lead to social isolation for some children and the loss of self-esteem and confidence may be another outcome.

The impact on behaviour can be very variable but children in poverty may lack guidance because of the stressful nature of their family life and this may result in difficult behaviour inside and outside the family. The effect of poverty on self-esteem and confidence may result in aggressive and hostile behaviour and poor relationships with peers. Stress may make children in poverty find some events and situations hard to manage and may reduce effective development of problem-solving skills.

Social and Cultural Background

Children in early years settings come from a range of different cultural backgrounds which have shaped their experiences and learning in their early years in different ways. Cultural norms and beliefs, behaviour and attitudes will influence how a child sees the environment and behaves in response to his experiences in that environment. These experiences and the child's responses may vary a great deal according to the social and cultural expectations the child has learned about from birth. For some children, there may be a much closer match between cultural expectations within the early years setting and from early years practitioners than there is for other children. Children from ethnic minority groups may in particular find that expectations and experiences in the early years setting are bewilderingly different from those in their home environment.

Social groups may also differ in terms of behaviour and expectations of children and this may make for wide variation in the types of behaviour children have learned in the home. This is not necessarily a value-judgement, in that differences in behaviour may be a product of different social values and should not always be judged as 'better' or 'worse'. Social values have changed over time as discussed above and behaviours in children such as presenting their own views and opinions, negotiating, and disagreeing with adult expectations may be more acceptable now than they used to be.

However, different behaviours may be more accepted within rather than between social groups. Children may not have a problem with this until they come into contact with other social behaviours, different to their own. The first time this may happen to many children is when they enter an early years setting. As such, some children risk having behaviour that is seen as acceptable in the home and possibly community being poorly received in their early years setting.

Changing Family Types and Composition

The range of family types has widened considerably over the last 50 years with many children now experiencing more than one type during their childhoods. This diversity of family types also reflects changing notions of what a family is, making defining 'the family' increasingly difficult. Not all families involve married parents and many families are highly complex with interconnected branches linked by marriage, co-parenting and both biological and non-biological ties.

Around half of children born today are born to non-married couples. This does not mean that all these children are raised by single parents. Many couples cohabit before marriage and some children live in stable two-parent households where parents never marry. A snapshot of the breakdown of family types at any one time will only give part of the picture. Although children may be growing up as part of a single parent family during one period of their childhood, most single parents remarry or cohabit again becoming stepfamilies or blended families.

Young children are more likely now to experience changes such as the divorce and separation of parents, which may influence behaviour both within and outside the home. Divorce in itself may not necessarily be problematical, especially if it brings a stressful period of parental disharmony to an end. However, divorce and separation are often accompanied by loss of income and extended family and a change of home and school, friends and familiar environments. Parents may have less time and energy for children during separations and parenting styles may become less responsive. Accommodating stepsiblings and new half-siblings, stepparents and new extended family members may also be stressful for children.

New technologies, attitudes and cultural developments have resulted in more different types of families. More children now live in same-sex parent families with lesbian or gay parents, which may bring stresses for the child when family types are compared. Despite the increasing diversity in family types, the married heterosexual couple family with their own biological children is still upheld as the 'gold standard' and children whose family life does not conform to this may feel stigmatized.

It is also important to remember that some children

may have suffered significant losses of family, including children who have been bereaved, the many children who lose contact with fathers after separation or divorce and adopted and fostered children. Children who have lost parental contact for any reason may suffer from feelings of sadness and loss, anger at their abandonment or bewilderment and failure to understand what has happened to them. This may be reflected in a range of behaviours depending on the child's age and stage of development, personal characteristics, the circumstances of the loss and the extent to which the child's feelings are recognized and responded to by carers.

Child Abuse

Cleaver, Unell and Aldgate (1999) identified domestic abuse, drug and alcohol abuse and mental health problems as factors having a significant negative impact on parenting and, as such, as being implicated in child abuse. Children living in households where more than one of these factors are present are more likely to suffer abuse and/or neglect. The extent to which these factors impact on children's development depends on the combination and duration of the problems.

The best predictor of adverse long-term effects on

children is the coexistence of mental illness or problem drinking with family disharmony.
                        (Cleaver, Unell and Aldgate, 1999: 23)

Child abuse is prevalent in all age groups of children, but
government statistics for England show that children in
the early years are most vulnerable. Those aged 1–5
make up 30 per cent of abused children; those aged 5–9
constitute another 31 per cent and babies under one
another 8 per cent (DfES, March 2004).

The abuse of children can have both short- and long-
term negative effects on children's health and well-
being. The extent to which these effects impede the
child's developmental progress depends on the duration, severity and types of abuse the child experiences,
the child's age at the time of the abuse and the child's
own level of resilience (Kay, 2003a). Child abuse may
also have other negative effects on children who may
have to leave their homes, be separated from significant
others including siblings and parents, and who may
experience feelings of guilt and anxiety about their role
in abuse coming to light. Children may also have to go
through distressing medical examinations and inter-
views with police and social workers.

Abuse often takes place in the context of poor-quality
parenting, lack of warmth and sensitivity to the child
and inconsistent controls. The child may lack support
for her overall developmental progress within the

family and she may witness violence to other family members. Children who have been abused may have poor-quality attachments to others and find it difficult to make meaningful relationships. They commonly have developmental delays and may have suffered physical injury. Abused children usually experience long- or short-term emotional problems and problems making relationships with adults and other children. They may be traumatized by their experiences or unable to make sense of what has happened to them. Almost universally, abused children have significant issues with self-esteem (Kay, 2003a).

One of the key difficulties for abused children is that the outcomes for them often mean that their behaviour results in further rejections and social failures. They tend to find it difficult to regulate their feelings or behaviour and may be aggressive or over dependent with others. They may behave more immaturely than peers and many abused children will regress to less mature stages of behaviour. When faced with difficult situations, their lack of coping strategies mean that they react inappropriately, alienating others. Lack of empathy and poor understanding of others' feelings and motivations may also exacerbate the problems abused children face in social situations. Abused children may also experience discontinuity in learning and education and may have lacked a cognitively stimulating environment in their earliest years, meaning that it is very common for abused children to have some form of learning difficulty or delays (Kay, 2003b).

Jon and Kev

Some abused children may repeat the behaviour of adults around them and, depending on the type of abuse, may behave in unacceptable ways towards other children and adults. Their behaviour could be modelled on the adults' or it could be a way of drawing attention to the abuse. It may be that the abuse has been such a part of the child's formative experiences that he does not recognize that the behaviours involved are not acceptable. Many abused children may have behavioural problems that lead to further difficulties for them.

Jon, 8, and Kev, 6, were the two oldest children in a family of five where all the children were subjected to physical, emotional and sexual abuse. Jon was placed with foster carers who found it very difficult to care for him because of his sexualized awareness and behaviour towards the mother in the family. She complained that he 'leered' at her and that she could not give him a hug without him touching her inappropriately. His teacher agreed, saying that Jon made sexual comments and looked at her in unacceptable ways when in the class. She was uncomfortable around him and did not like to be alone with him. Kev had been emotionally abused and rejected by his parents and was very disturbed by the move to foster care. Kev attacked another child in the playground, grabbing his genitals and threatening further sexual assault. The child's parents were incensed,

---

describing Kev as a 'pervert' and a 'monster'. They wanted him excluded from the school for their own child's safety.

Discussion Points

1. What strategies might work to support more acceptable behaviour from Jon?
2. How do you think the school should handle the incident with Kev in the short-term and support his behavioural development in the longer term?

Summary and Conclusions

In this chapter, some of the social and environmental influences on children's behaviour have been discussed and the ways in which these factors interact have been examined through the use of ecological models. Different types of parenting have been discussed in terms of their possible effect on children's development and behaviour, and some of the influences on parenting approach have been outlined.

It is important to remember that the influences discussed will have a different effect on parenting approaches and children's development and behaviour depending on many factors. The extent of support for the child and family, the age and stage of development of the child, the relationship between the child and family and the personal characteristics of the child and parents that can determine resilience or vulnerability, are all significant. As such, practitioners should be careful to avoid assumptions about the impact of particular events or environmental or social conditions on the behaviour of a child or family.

In the next chapter, the impact of disabilities and learning difficulties or delays on children's behaviour is discussed.

3 The Impact of Developmental Differences on Behaviour

The links between a child's developmental stage and progress and their behaviour have already been discussed. For some children, impairments or delays in development may have a significant impact on how they behave and this in turn may influence the parenting approach used in their homes and the response of other adults to the child. On the other hand, children who have disabilities or learning difficulties may react to an environment in which they feel alienated and 'different' by behaving in unacceptable ways if the support they receive is insufficient to enable them to cope.

In this chapter, the relationship between disabilities and other developmental issues and behavioural problems will be discussed with reference to meeting all children's needs and dealing with behavioural issues in a developmental context. Some of the responses practitioners could make to the child's behaviour are discussed. Developing an inclusive setting to meet all children's needs is discussed in Chapter 4. Responding to individual behaviour is discussed in Chapter 6.

The term 'developmental issues' will be used as a broad reference to the types of developmental delays, impairments or differences that may require the child to need additional support in learning and other aspects of development. A 'disability' is a term used to describe specific impairments to the child's development, which are diagnosed and recognized. 'Learning difficulties' relates to children who have delays or problems in their learning but are not described as disabled. Children with 'special educational needs' (SEN) are those defined as needing extra support to access the curriculum successfully. Needless to say, these definitions overlap considerably.

Links between Developmental Issues and Behaviour

There is evidence that children with special educational needs are over-represented among disruptive children in educational settings, including early years centres, and there are links between disruptive behaviour and poor language skills and slow literacy development also. In early years settings alone, children with poor language skills and social skills and limited concentration were found to be more likely to have behavioural problems (Ofsted, March 2005).

Roffey (2004) suggested the following categories for children with learning difficulties who also had behavioural problems:

♦ they are developing at a slower pace than other students;

♦ they have a specific difficulty, especially in literacy skills, where they consistently fail to meet the expectations of others;

♦ they do not understand the language of instruction;

♦ they have unmet emotional needs or are experiencing great distress which impinges on their ability to learn;

♦ they are not skilled in paying attention to teacher input and have a fragmented concentration on set tasks;

♦ they are more able than their peers and either are trying to 'fit in' or are under-stimulated in class.

(Roffey, 2004: 97)

There may be many different explanations for the child's learning difficulties, but effectively the link between these and behavioural problems comes about because the child is struggling, or in some cases failing, to cope with the learning environment, the curriculum and others within the setting.

Schopler (1995) developed the 'Iceberg' analogy to demonstrate the relationship between behavioural problems and the child's impairments for children with autism. However, this model could be used to demonstrate this relationship for all children with disabilities and learning difficulties. The visible part of the 'iceberg' is the specific behaviour, as shown in Fig. 3.1. However, the invisible parts of the 'iceberg' are the underlying impairments that shape or cause the child's behaviour. Understanding this relationship is the key to recognizing

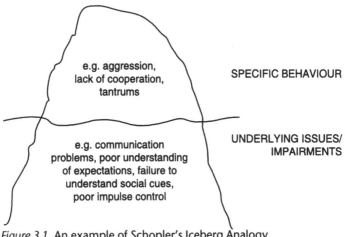

Figure 3.1 An example of Schopler's Iceberg Analogy

the roots of a child's difficult behaviour and working to help the child with these, rather than merely responding to the behaviour.

Impairments or delays in development may come about for a number of reasons. Children may be born with disabilities affecting development or acquire these through accident or illness. Children may be diagnosed with specific conditions such as autistic spectrum disorders or Attention Deficit and Hyperactivity Disorder. Some developmental delays and learning difficulties are caused by the quality of care children receive in their early years, particularly noticeable in children who are in public care or placed for adoption, where early abuse and neglect and subsequent changes of carers have negatively influenced the child's holistic development.

The relationship between disability and learning difficulties and behavioural issues is not straightforward. Children do not automatically behave unacceptably because they are disabled or have a learning difficulty. In some cases a developmental issue creates stresses for a child that may affect behaviour. In other cases the developmental issue may lead to behaviour that is more difficult for adults to understand and manage. In an early years setting, the issue may be that the child's behaviour is different to her peers and therefore harder to manage in a group situation where expectations of the children are uniform.

Ben

Ben, 7, has significant problems with reading and writing which have been described as dyslexia by his educational psychologist. He receives some additional support in class to help with his work. He is a bright child who is good at history, geography and science. Ben is also dyspraxic and attends a course of physiotherapy delivered in school to support the development of his fine and gross motor skills. Ben is conscious of being 'different' to other children and very frustrated by his inability to easily access literacy skills. He describes himself as 'stupid' and his self-esteem is poor despite the efforts of his parents, teacher and teaching assistant to encourage and support him.

Ben's low self-esteem impacts on his relationships with other children. Although he has social skills, Ben finds it difficult to join in some games, as his physical coordination is poor. He lacks confidence about approaching other children and sees himself as having few friends and not being popular. Ben has occasional angry outbursts at school, particularly in the playground. He can be aggressive with other children and he gets into fights. He can also be aggressive at home, and he has physically attacked his mother and sister.

Discussion Points

1. What are the influences on Ben's behaviour?
2. What approaches may help Ben with his behaviour?

The Impact of Developmental Differences

Some examples of the types of disabilities and learning difficulties that may affect behaviour are discussed below, although it is important to remember that this list is far from complete and the distinctions between the sections may be artificial. For example, communication difficulties may be found as a specific problem for a child or as part of a more complex disorder such as Asperger syndrome.

It is important to recognize that children's behaviour may vary to a great extent in response to a particular developmental issue depending on the child's characteristics and ability to adapt, and the quality and extent of support the child receives at home and in the setting. In some cases, behavioural issues are a product not just of the child's response to his or developmental issue, but because of inappropriate or unhelpful adult reactions to the child or lack of appropriate support for the child's difficulties.

Communication Skills

Children may have delays in speech or language development, impaired language development or may be required to learn in a second language. Some children may have articulation problems (difficulties in forming sounds) and others may have hearing impairment.

Other children may be able to hear words but have problems in comprehending the meanings of others' speech or nonverbal communications. Communication is a key factor in all aspects of cognitive development and in social development, making friends and taking part in group and individual learning activities. Children with communication difficulties may find accessing play and other activities extraordinarily difficult and frustrating. They may find it hard to make friends, share ideas and have fun. Learning may be delayed if a child has speech and language delays that limit conversation or understanding of instructions or content of teaching.

Language development is closely linked to other forms of development and a child may have problems in developing cognitively if they have limited 'inner speech' (through which children explain things to themselves and develop their thoughts and ideas.) The ability to develop skills in play, particularly socio-dramatic play, is also dependent on language as children develop shared play themes through conversation. The role of play in children's wider development is highly significant in the early years, but children with communication difficulties may gain limited benefits from all forms of play without high levels of support. Children with hearing impairments may find it difficult to hear the differences between sounds and this may impact on their literacy development.

For some children, communication is difficult in the

early years because they are required to communicate in spoken English, which may not be their first language. Children may have another first spoken language or they may communicate primarily in sign languages such as British Sign Language or Makaton.

The impact of communication difficulties on behaviour can be very variable depending on the child and the type of communication problem she faces. However, communication problems can result in:

- frustration and anger;
- aggression;
- non-compliance;
- emotional upsets, distress and weeping;
- withdrawal from adults and children;
- refusal to join in with play or other activities;
- reluctance to enter the setting.

In order to support a child with communication difficulties, practitioners should:

- ensure that they are clear about what the child's difficulty entails;
- know what support the child has at home and what strategies are used to help the child communicate;

♦ ensure there are strategies in place to support the child effectively;

♦ ensure that all those involved with the child are aware of these strategies and are implementing them;

♦ review the child's progress and needs regularly;

♦ seek expert advice on effective strategies;

♦ be prepared to talk to parents about referring the child for support from other agencies;

♦ be aware of the impact of the communication difficulty on all aspects of the child's learning and other development including social aspects;

♦ work with the whole group of children to help them support the child and to ensure that he is not bullied or excluded;

♦ be prepared to support the child's self-esteem on an ongoing basis.

Children with Learning Disabilities or Delays

Children may have learning disabilities or delays for many different reasons. These may include specific conditions, such as Down's syndrome, or it may be that the

Dave

It is important to remember that even children with mild communication problems may have significant difficulties unless the support they receive is effective. A child faced with problems that may make him feel different, lose self-esteem and find the learning process difficult and frustrating may develop behavioural responses to his situation that signal that he is struggling. Ignoring these signals may result in further behavioural difficulties and possibly learning delays.

Dave, 4, has below-average hearing because of a series of ear infections in his babyhood. He has regular hearing tests but does not need to use a hearing aid. Dave is in Foundation Stage 2 in a small primary school. Dave cannot always hear what is said to him in a noisy crowded room and sometimes he does not hear instructions, which makes him anxious and upset. Dave cannot differentiate between sounds very well and regularly mixes up similar sounds such as 'b' and 'p'. In general, Dave has quite good language skills but he sometimes mispronounces new words because he has misheard them and he often misses off the first sound of new words. For example, he says 'out' for 'without'. Dave has started to refuse to do certain types of activities, especially those that focus on sounds, and he has become withdrawn and uncooperative on occasion. He has also become very sensitive to comments from other children about his verbal mistakes and has become angry and distressed about this. It is noticeable that Dave is often

> alone at playtime and that he sometimes ignores approaches from other children.
>
> **Discussion Points**
>
> 1. What support might be most effective to help Dave with his learning?
> 2. What social support would help Dave feel more part of the group and make friends?

child's early environment, social and parenting experiences have led to delays. Delays are common in children who are in public care, many of whom have suffered abuse or neglect and may have had several changes of placement and carers in their short lives. Learning disabilities may be general, affecting all aspects of the child's ability to learn, or specific, affecting a particular aspect of learning. One of the most common specific learning disabilities is dyslexia, which affects the child's ability to learn and use literacy skills but does not necessarily affect other aspects of learning such as verbal skills.

Learning disabilities may be mild, moderate or severe. Some children may have the capacity to 'catch up' with their learning in a supportive environment while others may have conditions that permanently limit their ability to learn. For some children, learning may be difficult not because there are problems with cognitive functioning but because of social and communication difficulties.

The Impact of Developmental Differences

For example, children with Asperger's or nonverbal learning difficulties may have the potential to learn cognitively, but social and communication problems associated with these conditions may result in limited learning.

For all children with learning disabilities or delays, key factors are frustration in dealing with the learning process and social issues related to being 'different.' Learning delays or disabilities may result in:

♦ frustration, anger and distress with the learning process;

♦ challenging behaviour designed to distract from the learning process;

♦ refusal to be involved in learning activities;

♦ non-compliance;

♦ aggression, attention seeking behaviour and distraction of other children from the task at hand;

♦ poor concentration, restlessness and lack of application;

♦ low self-esteem, problems with peers, social exclusion.

In order to support the child with learning disabilities or delays, practitioners should:

+ make sure they have clear and detailed information about the child's needs;

+ have good communication with parents about how to support the child's learning and behaviour;

+ have good communication with other professionals involved with the child and family;

+ ensure the curriculum is differentiated to meet the child's needs and that the child can access the learning taking place;

+ have strategies in place to support the child's self-esteem and social status;

+ have a whole-group strategy to ensure the child is included in play and friendship groups;

+ ensure that behavioural expectations are as high for the child as for all children in the group.

Jane

Children with learning disabilities may find early years settings daunting places, especially if they have social problems which make them struggle with some aspects of the setting. Jane, 6, has nonverbal learning disability that affects her physical ability and confidence, communication skills, social skills and ability to learn in some areas. While Jane can read quite well, she has problems understanding and interpreting what she has read. She can follow instructions for science experiments but has problems explaining what the results may mean.

Jane's relationships with other children are poor. Although Jane is verbal, she has a poor understanding of social cues and nonverbal communication so it is difficult for her to 'match' her responses to another child's communications. Often she 'talks across' others or responds inappropriately to what they say.

Jane's learning seems to be more problematical now that it was a year ago. As more abstract, interpretative thinking is required in her learning she struggles more to keep up.

Action Points

1. Look up nonverbal learning difficulties on the Internet and make notes of the problems children with this diagnosis experience.
2. Find information on the sites you access to provide some ideas about how you could support Jane in her learning and social development.

Attention Deficit and Hyperactivity Disorder (ADHD) and ADD

These conditions are related but different, in that children with ADHD are hyperactive and inattentive, while children with ADD are not hyperactive but are inattentive (Porter, 2003). Children with these disorders are usually diagnosed in early childhood. Key factors in the disorders are impulsivity, inattention and, in ADHD, hyperactivity. Children with these disorders commonly have learning difficulties, concentration problems, poor emotional state, difficulties in self-organizing and controlling their own behaviour, and problems with relationships inside and beyond the family. They may be physically and verbally aggressive and this can affect relationships with others and socially isolate the child. ADHD in particular can be extremely stressful for the family who may become emotionally and physically exhausted by an aggressive, hyperactive child.

ADHD/ADD have been controversial because of the rapidly rising numbers of children who are diagnosed, particularly in the US, and the use of drugs to control the symptoms. In addition, ADHD/ADD may be hard to diagnose with no simple diagnosis or assessment approach. However, many diagnosticians are now using a checklist and formula for assessing children that takes into account the range of symptoms and the impact of the child's behaviour on home and other settings. In some cases, ADHD and ADD are treated with medication, although the benefits of medicating young children with these disorders have been challenged, and medication is considered only one of the strategies for supporting such children. ADHD and ADD may result in:

- aggression and angry uncontrolled behaviour around other children;
- social isolation;
- inability to concentrate or settle to a task;
- poor impulse control;
- inappropriate, defiant behaviour;
- poor organization and ability to follow instructions.

In order to support a child with ADHD or ADD, practitioners should:

- ensure the child is diagnosed and support arrangements have been agreed in partnership with parents and other involved agencies;
- give instructions in short sections and repeat as necessary;
- help the child develop organization skills;
- support the child's social development and teach self-control strategies;
- work with parents and acknowledge their high stress levels and possible self-blame.

Marcus

Marcus is 4. He is currently in nursery but about to move into Foundation Stage 2. Marcus has been diagnosed as having ADHD. He has poor concentration and finds it almost impossible to sit down for long. He fidgets and interrupts others, sometimes shouting out when he wants attention. Marcus often finds it difficult to join in activities because he finds it hard to pay attention to instructions. He flits from one thing to another and often disrupts other children's play or activities. If they protest he can become angry and shout at them, and on occasion he has lost his temper and pushed other children roughly. The staff in the nursery are concerned that Marcus will start to struggle more as he progresses through school as he has shown no interest in developing literacy or numeracy skills to date.

Action Point

Research into the needs of children with ADHD in school and draw up a plan for supporting Marcus in his transition to Foundation Stage 2.

Children with Autistic Spectrum Disorders

The term autistic spectrum disorders (ASD) covers a number of related conditions that affect up to 520,000 children and adults in the UK (Action for ASD, 2005).

The Impact of Developmental Differences

Children with ASD are identified by a triad of areas of impairment that are common to all but which may have been apparent to differing extents depending on the type of autism. The areas of impairment are:

♦ Social interaction – impaired understanding of non-verbal communication; problems with making and keeping friendships; lack of interest in others; socially unresponsive.

♦ Communication – delays or impairment in language development; may not initiate or sustain conversation; repetitive language use.

♦ Imagination – lack of flexibility; restricted, repetitive patterns of behaviour, interests and activities; lack of imaginative or symbolic play.

Levels of ability vary, with children with some forms of ASD, such as Asperger syndrome, having better communication skills, and other children at the extreme end of the spectrum not developing language at all. Children can be diagnosed as young as 18 months old, but the average age for diagnosis is 5 years (Action for ASD, 2005). As with ADHD/ADD, autistic disorders are more common in boys, with a 4:1 ratio of boys to girls being generally agreed.

Behavioural problems in children with ASD may include:

- angry outbursts;
- non-compliance with requests;
- non-communication;
- making rude or inappropriate remarks or noises;
- running away;
- overreacting to trivial incidents;
- refusing to join in activities.

In order to support a child with ASD, the practitioner could:

- use social stories to explain rules or requirements;
- divide tasks into small steps and make sure instructions are written;
- give clear verbal instructions;
- provide the child with a place for 'time out' for when he becomes distressed;
- place boundaries or limitations on the duration and timing of obsessive behaviour but do not try to stop this altogether;
- plan cooperative activities such as paired work or teamwork sensitively and prepare the child for this.

Brian

Brian, 8, has Asperger syndrome. He has attended a mainstream primary school since he was 5. He was diagnosed when he was 6, after mounting concerns about his 'odd' behaviour. Brian has started to curl in a foetal position in the playground when he feels threatened by other children during breaks and he has increasingly disrupted lessons by shouting, banging on the desk and humming loudly. He refuses to enter the hall for assembly, covering his ears and complaining that it is too noisy. Although he has had friends in the past, Brian's increasingly difficult behaviour has started to socially isolate him. It is clear that Brian is a bright child but he often refuses to do tasks in school and he will not read or do homework outside school.

Discussion Points

1. Write a plan to go in Brian's Individual Education Plan (IEP) for supporting him with his behaviour.
2. If you are unsure of whether you know enough about Asperger syndrome, look at some of the websites listed at the end of the book.

Summary and Conclusions

In this chapter, some of the developmental issues for children that may affect behaviour have been discussed with reference to some specific disabilities. The links between development and behaviour have been explored along with the types of reactions children may have when they are struggling to cope. Some of the more helpful responses were outlined in relation to different types of disabilities. However, it is important to remember that the discussion above only gives examples of a small number of developmental issues affecting children. The range of issues and disabilities, which may influence development and behaviour, is very much wider.

Supporting children to cope with the areas which are difficult for them in terms of their development is a key strategy in behaviour management. This is discussed further in subsequent chapters.

4 Supporting Positive
Behavioural Development

In this chapter, strategies for creating environments which promote positive behavioural development in children are discussed. This chapter focuses on the general promotion and management of behaviour in a developmental context and a whole-setting approach, rather than the management of individual behaviour, which is discussed in Chapter 6. This notion of promoting positive behaviour in children encompasses the behaviour and attitudes of adults in the setting, the ethos and values underpinning approaches to early years care and education, and the place of behaviour development in the curriculum. The chapter also addresses issues of creating an inclusive environment to meet the needs of all children.

If we accept the premise that children's behaviour is often responsive, then creating a supportive environment for children's development is a means to reducing incidents of negative or harmful behaviour. If we agree with Porter's (2003) view that children's behaviour is a developmental area rather than something to control through rewards and punishments, then it is logical that settings should give thought and attention to how children's behavioural development can be supported alongside other aspects of their development.

However, a key element in promoting positive behaviour is working in partnership. Partnership with colleagues in the setting provides the opportunity to develop skills and attitudes, strategies and innovations in behaviour management. Although early years practitioners can take important steps as individuals to improve their immediate work environment in terms of promoting positive behaviour, a whole-setting approach provides an effective framework for success in this area.

Another key issue to consider is the extent to which early years settings can alone make a difference to children's behavioural development. Parents have the key role in their children's overall development and children spend the majority of their time in the home environment. Working with parents to support children's development is the most effective way forward. Partnership with parents in this area will achieve better results, as is the case in most aspects of children's care, education and holistic development. Partnerships with other agencies are also key elements to success in developing effective strategies for promoting positive behaviour.

Although the individual practitioner has a key role in promoting positive behaviour, this can only be effective if it is part of a wider strategy within the setting. Behaviour management strategies need to be envisaged, developed and implemented at the whole-setting level and involve all staff, children and parents in order to be effective.

The Whole-Setting Approach

A whole-setting approach is one that encompasses the behaviour and attitudes of all members of the setting community. It is not just about what the children are expected to do but also about adult roles and responsibilities, relationships and attitudes, management structures and leadership, and communication within and outside the setting. Rogers (2000) advocates a 'whole-school' approach to behaviour management that is based on change management and collaborative responses within the setting. He argues that the benefits of whole-setting approaches are:

♦ less stress for staff;

♦ reduced incidents of disruptive behaviour;

♦ better structures for supporting staff dealing with disruptive behaviour;

♦ staff feeling better supported within a collaborative environment.

Whole-setting approaches involve a number of inter-related activities that combine to support improvements in the environment in terms of support for positive behaviour. These activities could include:

♦ a collaborative approach to the development of a behaviour management policy;

♦ management responsibility for creating the ethos to support approaches to managing behaviour;

♦ a responsive, supportive environment for staff to develop behaviour management strategies within;

♦ clear responses to concerns or ideas about how to develop better approaches to behaviour;

♦ relevant training including skills development for communicating with children.

Whole-setting approaches are very much concerned with creating environments in which reactions to unwanted behaviour are only a part of behaviour management. In the first place, settings should be creating environments that 'prevent and minimize' unwanted behaviour (Rogers, 2000: 22). Weare (2004: 53) argues that whole-school approaches are needed to develop emotionally literate schools because 'analyses and solutions that work in practice are usually holistic ones'. Emotionally literate settings are those that strongly promote support for children's emotional and social development and where positive behavioural developments are seen as a product of this.

In this chapter, the concept of whole-setting approaches will underpin the discussion about how to promote positive behaviour in children.

Determining What Sort of Behaviour is Wanted

Promoting positive behaviour depends on what we see as 'positive'. In the first place, behavioural expectations of children are not value free. They reflect cultural and individual expectations and they are based on some form of view about how we want children to behave. These views may well change over time as behavioural standards change or ideas and expectations about how children learn best develop. In the past, behavioural standards have been quite different to those now. In the author's childhood, children were not expected to speak in class unless they were invited to answer a question, and they certainly were not allowed to work together on projects or discuss their work with other children.

Managing Behaviour in the Early Years

As briefly discussed in Chapter 1, one of the issues that settings need to work on is to develop a common understanding of what types of behaviour are wanted. Often behaviour management focuses on unwanted behaviour, but this can leave children bewildered as to what we do want them to do. Inconsistencies can be very confusing to children, where different members of staff have different expectations of them. Developing a view on behavioural standards within the setting needs to involve staff and also parents and children to ensure that the key stakeholders within the setting agree on what those standards should be.

Involving Children:
One of the main benefits of involving children in this process is to help them understand the reasoning behind 'rules' and expectations and to ensure that they are involved and have a stake in promoting positive behaviour. Fisher (2002) argues that power and control within the setting needs to be negotiated between practitioners and children in order to motivate the children and to help them become active participants in their own learning. In the absence of other means, children often learn about the routines and rules in a setting through imitation (Fisher, 2002). Although this may help children learn how to behave in particular situations, it may not support their behavioural development. The children may not learn about or internalize

behavioural standards because they do not learn what these are from merely imitating behaviour. As with any other area of learning, children benefit from having input into behavioural development through:

♦ understanding the reasons for behavioural standards;

♦ negotiating what those standards should be and having ownership of them;

♦ being active rather than passive in this process;

♦ being treated as 'competent learners'.

Through this approach, practitioners have to relinquish some of their control of what happens in this area. This approach relates to Porter's ideas about our need to trust children to develop in their behaviour without having to exercise excessive controls on this process through rewards and punishments (2003).

Children can be involved in developing behavioural standards through:

♦ participation in discussion about expectations;

♦ developing 'rules' for the group or setting;

♦ school councils;

♦ circle time.

It is important to give young children time to develop

their ideas about behavioural standards and to discuss these. Young children may need guidance on what will work in practice but conversations about principles of behaviour can be surprisingly fruitful. Themes that can be useful to form a basis for discussion are:

♦ What sort of behaviour makes everyone happy?

♦ Why is it important to make everyone happy?

♦ What behaviours make others sad or upset?

♦ What should we do if someone forgets about positive behaviour?

♦ What sorts of things might lead someone forget to behave positively?

It is also important to remember that children are still developing behaviourally and that, as in every other aspect of development, they may make mistakes and need guidance.

Involving Parents:
Involving parents in developing behavioural standards is also important. In every household there will be different rules and expectations of children and there will be different responses to unwanted behaviour. Early years settings need to promote their values to parents, but also to share parents' ideas and values about positive

behaviour and how to promote this. One of the main areas of problems for children in this area is when behavioural expectations in the setting and at home are very different. Parents may welcome the opportunity to discuss behavioural standards and to share ideas about supporting positive behaviour. In situations where parents may be struggling to promote positive behaviour in the home, settings may be able to provide a considerable amount of support for developing this effectively through modelling good practice and effective strategies. Some settings may provide parenting support through individual advice and discussion or through parenting classes. Much of this focuses on positive behaviour management approaches and child-centred disciplinary methods.

To ensure parents are involved in developing behavioural standards:

♦ make sure the behaviour management policy is available for parents to read and comment on;

♦ give parents material or discuss with them the philosophy underpinning the behaviour development strategy in the setting;

♦ get parents involved in reviewing the behaviour management policy;

♦ encourage parents to discuss setting 'rules' and to share ideas about these;

♦ explain to parents how children are involved in discussions about behavioural standards;

♦ invite parents to come and work with children on particular topics that may interest them.

However, it is also important to be sure that communication about behaviour is two-way. Parents often have effective strategies for dealing with behaviour that they can share with practitioners and, as in all aspects of their children's development, should be acknowledged as 'experts' in their own child.

Involving Practitioners:
Approaches to behaviour management should be considered as a regular agenda item in meetings and an area for discussion and management development. Practitioners should have opportunity to be involved in developing policy in the setting and they should have access to relevant training to support their own development in this area. It is important to staff to have access to additional resources when faced with new behavioural challenges. It can be very helpful to get advice and support from other agencies when new challenges arise. For example, one private day nursery sent a staff member on a social services course for working with children with disabilities when their first child with Down's syndrome was admitted to the setting. The

parents were concerned that the child was not always responsive to requests and the practitioner wanted to be able to understand what the child's needs might be and to be able to respond effectively to these.

A setting that is clear about behavioural standards

Extending Knowledge and Understanding

When Adam transferred to Year 2 in a new primary school his parents explained that he was an adopted child with attachment issues that affected his behaviour and relationships with others. The teacher found that Adam was an intellectually gifted child who found it difficult to engage with the work and other activities in the class. He could be very disruptive at times, interfering with other children's activities and wandering around the room at will. Adam could also become very withdrawn and would cease to communicate with others. When his teacher tried to influence his behaviour, such as persuading him to stop poking other children on his table, Adam would become instantly unresponsive and uncooperative.

Despite several discussions with Adam's parents, the teacher did not feel he had sufficient knowledge and skills to understand and manage this behaviour successfully. After consultation with the SENCO, it was arranged for a psychologist from the local Child and Adolescent Mental Health Services (CAMHS) to come and do some training and offer advice on children with attachment disorders to staff in the school.

Discussion Points

1. How would this issue have been dealt with in your setting?
2. What sort of support do you think may be recommended for Adam in school?

should be publishing these, discussing these and promoting these through aspects of the curriculum. Behavioural standards should encompass the behaviour of all members of the early years community, not just focus entirely on the children's behaviour. They should be stated positively and they should be developed and supported by all members of the setting community. The development of behaviour management policies is discussed in more detail in Chapter 5.

What Factors Support Positive Behavioural Development?

The Ofsted report *Managing Challenging Behaviour* (March 2005) looks at some of the issues that are significant in early years and other settings in terms of best practice for creating an environment for successful behaviour management. Key recommendations include the following:

♦ focus on improving the quality of teaching and the provision of an appropriate curriculum that engages pupils and meets their needs;

♦ do more to improve the literacy and other communication skills of pupils with difficult behaviour;

♦ improve systems for tracking academic and social development, and make better use of this information to help pupils improve and manage their behaviour;

♦ provide more systematic training for senior managers, teachers and assistants in behaviour management and in child development;

♦ review ways of linking with parents;

♦ underline the need for consistency among staff in the way expectations of behaviour are set and maintained.

Perhaps most significantly, with reference to the first point, the report suggests that a key factor is ensuring that the curriculum is accessible for all children by adapting it to meet the range of needs within the group.

The key elements within these findings are represented in Fig. 4.1, which demonstrates some of the links between the different factors.

Clearly, the elements within a strategy to promote positive behaviour do not operate independently but are

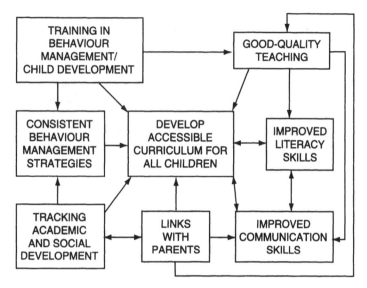

Figure 4.1 Key Elements of a Strategy to Promote Positive Behaviour

interrelated and co-dependent. In addition, there are underpinning factors that need to be considered in order for the strategy to be successful. These are as follows:

♦ individual children's needs must be recognized and met both in terms of their learning and their social and emotional development;

♦ good-quality communication with the child, parents, within the early years staff group and with other relevant agencies is vital;

106

- high standards of leadership are required to ensure effective implementation of a behaviour management strategy;

- training in behaviour management is needed for all staff.

The suggested strategy involves a wide range of different areas of change or improvement in the setting. In order to consider these in a more manageable way, the following sections look at some practical approaches to achieving these changes and/or maintaining good standards in early years settings.

Practitioner Behaviour and Attitudes

In any early years setting, practitioners act as role models to the children in their care. Young children learn a great deal of their behaviour from imitating others, using close observation and mimicry to develop their skills. Children have to learn quite a lot to be able to distinguish between the types of behaviour they learn from others. They do not have the skills, in their early years, to distinguish between behaviours it is helpful to learn and repeat and those that should be avoided. Yet adults often seem to take children's powers to discriminate between behaviours they should emulate and those they should not for granted. Children are not easily able to make those types of value-judgements and, even when they are beginning to understand some more general rules about behaviour, there is a strong incentive to repeat behaviour if an adult with authority and status in the child's view uses that behaviour. In slightly older children this process may be more self-conscious in the sense that, for example, the child may tell himself that if his father uses swearwords, so can he.

How adults behave in the setting is a key factor in determining children's behaviour. If practitioners regularly shout at children, children will shout. If the practitioner is rude and impatient, the children will be rude and impatient. If the practitioner fails to communicate clearly and carefully with children, then they will not develop good communication skills within the setting.

In order to promote positive behaviour in early years settings, adults need to consider their own behaviour

---

Getting the Adults to Behave

Children need to be able to see that behavioural standards apply to all, not just to them; otherwise they may resent or fail to understand the meaning of those standards. Adults need to be aware that their own behaviour is significant in terms of providing a role model for children.

A school council at a primary school had been discussing the problems of parking outside the school. Many parents arrived by car and parked briefly but sensibly. However, some double-parked, some pulled up on the zigzag lines and some more or less pushed their children out of the car as they paused in the middle of the road. The school council decided that this poor behaviour had to change. They placed a banner on the school gates announcing that adults who parked their cars on the zigzag lines were 'rude and dangerous' in protest at the constant flouting of safe parking behaviour by parents and other visitors to the school. They also wrote to the local council to ask for wider pavements to discourage parking right outside the school and were duly successful in getting these laid.

Discussion Points

1. How did this approach benefit the children and the school?
2. How would you have supported Year 1 pupils to contribute to this project?

and responses to children. The following characteristics of adult behaviour and attitudes are essential:

♦ respect and courtesy in dealing with all others;

♦ good communication;

♦ avoid shouting, expressions of anger or power-assertion;

♦ positive statements and attitudes towards others;

♦ empathy and sensitivity to others' needs;

♦ helpfulness and supportive behaviour;

♦ equity and fairness.

Case Studies of Practitioner Behaviour

Mr Smith teaches Year 2. He always uses a soft and gentle voice. He is cheerful and kind in his attitude and speaks to the children as if he likes and respects them. He shows pleasure in their company and responds thoughtfully and in a considered manner to their communications. When he comments on evidence of a child's learning, he is specific and gives details of areas where the child has developed and progress has been made. He deals with unwanted behaviour kindly and firmly by clearly stating what is expected but without confronting or humiliating the child. His classroom is calm and active, a hub of industry much of the time, and the children are engaged and intent on their learning.

Miss Taylor is a teaching assistant in the same small primary school. She is rather shy and lacking in confidence and some of the children she works with are aware of this. Miss Taylor sometimes gets ignored by the children and her instructions are sometimes not followed. When she asks unruly children to change their behaviour, this does not always happen. In some cases, this has led to escalation of behavioural problems that have led to children being sent out of the class or even to the head's office.

Miss Gainsborough is a nursery nurse in Foundation Stage 1 in the nursery attached to the school. She is quite fun and chatty with other staff and the children and she likes to gossip a bit and have 'a laugh' at work. She has favourites among the children and can be warm and friendly towards them. Miss Gainsborough does not always listen and respond to the children very consistently. She sets the planned activities up, but sometimes wanders off when she is supposed to be supporting a group or child. She does not often observe the children's behaviour and she sometimes makes negative comments to others about individual children she finds difficult.

Mrs Wood recently transferred from Year 6 to Year 2 teaching. She has a reputation for being fierce and used to shout very loudly at the Year 6 children. The Year 2 children were apprehensive about having her as a teacher because of this. Some of the younger boys in the class have been quite defiant with Mrs Wood. They have not followed instructions, defied her in front of the class and been disruptive, inattentive and rude. Mrs Wood's classes are sometimes uninspiring. The children spend a long time on whole-class activities and often they are on the carpet as a whole group for so long that they have all lost interest. Tasks and activities are repetitive and Mrs Wood gets annoyed with some children who ask for a lot of help.

Discussion Points

1. With reference to the discussion above, determine the factors that are effective or otherwise in each practitioner's approach.
2. What strategies might work in this school to improve standards of behaviour?

Support for Staff

The development of practitioners' skills in working effectively to minimize behavioural problems is not just the individual's responsibility. Settings need to promote skills development in practitioners through training and support for staff development within the context of a whole-setting strategy for development. This could include:

♦ training and staff development programmes;

♦ staff meetings that have behaviour management on the agenda;

♦ involving practitioners in developing policy;

♦ disseminating relevant research findings through the team;

♦ mentors to discuss behaviour management and give advice to newer staff.

Supporting Learning

Settings, and practitioners within these, need to consider the content and delivery of the curriculum, or activities in settings for 0–3 year olds, in order to determine how it will impact on children's behaviour. Young children's behaviour is often directly linked to the quality of their learning and other developmental experiences in the setting. It is clear that there is a strong link between promoting positive behaviour and the quality of the learning experiences children have (Ofsted, March 2005). *The Effective Provision of Pre-School Education (EPPE)* study confirmed that high-quality pre-school provision is significant in its positive effects on young children's intellectual, emotional and social behaviour (*EPPE*, 2003). The summary findings confirmed that in respect of children from disadvantaged backgrounds:

> The increased risk of anti-social/worried behaviour can be reduced by high-quality pre-school when they are aged 3 and 4.
>
> (*EPPE*, 2003: 3)

The findings also confirmed that this effect continued as

the young child went into school. The *EPPE* findings also found that improvements to practice were determined by:

- good curriculum knowledge;
- good understanding of child development;
- giving children formative feedback;
- a balance between adult- and child-initiated activities and play;
- effective behaviour management policies.

Bored, disengaged children; children who do not understand; children who understood it all days or even weeks ago; children who do not relate to the cultural basis of the activity; children who have better things to do than your activity – all of these have the potential for developing unwanted behaviour. Practitioners have a responsibility to ensure the curriculum is accessible, stimulating and engaging for all children. The *EPPE* findings also emphasized the importance of verbal interactions between adults and children to share and develop thinking and understanding, which they describe as 'sustained shared thinking'. Another key finding of the study was that in high-quality settings the content and delivery of the curriculum meets the needs of all children. No individual practitioner can provide high-quality provision for children alone in a group setting. The management ethos, principles and support for positive policies are crucial to ensuring that settings can achieve good standards.

In order to achieve this the following questions need to be considered:

+ Do the planned activities engage all the children and make sense to them?

+ Is the timing right or are children having to prematurely stop activities they are engaged in or carry on until they are bored?

+ Are the planned activities differentiated sufficiently to meet all children's needs?

+ Do the activities promote learning though exploration and investigation?

+ How is learning extended?

+ Do they build on themes that children have shown interest and engaged in?

+ Are the explanations and instructions clear?

+ Are individual children offered enough support and help to achieve?

+ Is there a good balance between practitioner-directed and child-directed activities?

♦ How is learning monitored and how are activities/ tasks evaluated in terms of their effectiveness in developing children's learning and engaging their interest?

In order to achieve good standards of teaching and learning in early years settings there needs to be a number of factors in place at individual and team levels:

♦ good teamwork and shared planning;

♦ sound knowledge and understanding of the curriculum;

♦ innovative and creative thinking;

♦ strategies for extending and building on learning;

♦ good understanding of differentiation and individual need;

♦ good levels of support for all children;

♦ effective monitoring and feedback systems to build into future planning.

Settings that are effective in developing positive behaviour also ensure that supporting the development of emotional and social skills is central to their work with children.

Supporting Emotional and Social Development

Supporting young children's emotional needs is a key factor in promoting their well-being and therefore their behaviour. Weare (2004) argues that developing emotional literacy in schools is linked to much-improved behavioural standards. She defines emotional literacy as:

> the ability to understand ourselves and other people, and in particular to be aware of, understand, and use information about the emotional states of ourselves and others with competence. It includes the ability to understand, express and manage our own emotions, and respond to the emotions of others, in ways that are helpful to ourselves and others.
>
> (2004: 2)

Strategies to promote emotional literacy can be central to improved inclusion for disruptive and difficult children, improving their social skills and the level of their acceptance in the group. Weare advocates a whole-school approach, in which a long-term developmental approach to work on emotional and social competences is 'high profile' (2004: 58).

Young children often take time to develop understanding of their own and others' emotions and their development in this area is very variable and cannot easily be judged by age. Individual children can also be variable in their emotional responses (as can we all) depending on circumstances, other events taking place in their lives, their physical state and whether they are having a 'good' day or not at that point. Many of the factors discussed in Chapter 2 that influence children's behaviour also affect their emotional state, and the influence of any of these factors present, the child's behaviour and her emotional state are inextricably interlinked.

Porter (2003: 3) lists children's emotional needs as follows:

- ◆ security;
- ◆ self-esteem;
- ◆ autonomy;
- ◆ belonging;
- ◆ fun;
- ◆ self-expression.

Reflection Point

Look back at the cases of Annie and Joe in Chapter 2, p. 35. For each child consider the following:

1. What do you think is the child's emotional state at the time?
2. To what extent are the child's emotional needs being met?
3. Which (if any) emotional needs may not be being met and why?

Choose one child in your setting at random. Over a week observe the child at different times and make notes on how the child's emotional needs are being met in the setting using Porter's list above as a checklist. In what ways (if any) are the child's needs not being met?

Children need their emotional needs met in order to:

♦ develop maturity, independence and autonomy;

♦ learn with confidence;

♦ develop social skills, friendships and rewarding relationships;

♦ regulate their emotional responses;

♦ respond to others' needs.

These are all important factors in children's behavioural development.

It is also important to remember that some children do not get all of their emotional needs met at home.

Children who are abused and neglected or who live in households high on criticism but low on warmth may have many unmet emotional needs. These may influence their behaviour in the early years setting and practitioners should be aware of factors that may be affecting children's emotional state in the short- and long-term.

Meeting Children's Emotional Needs

Amy is 6. Three weeks ago her mother had a heart attack. She is home now and recovering, but very limited in what she can do as yet. Amy's father is trying to care for his wife and the children and manage his own job at the same time. Despite help from friends and neighbours the whole family is exhausted and 'shell shocked'. Today Amy's friend tried on Amy's new gloves without asking her first. Amy hit her friend, threw the gloves on the floor and broke into uncontrollable floods of tears.

Harry is 4. He attends a private day-care centre as both parents work full time. His father usually picks Harry up but has not been for the last few weeks. Harry's mother has collected him but not stopped to chat and has looked very harassed, often snapping at Harry to hurry so she is not late to collect her older child from school. In this time, Harry has become weepy and uncooperative, seems very tired and unable to concentrate. He does not want to play with other children and has had regular tantrums over tiny issues. Harry's key worker cornered his mother today and spoke of her concerns about Harry. The mother burst into tears, saying this was the

---

last straw, she couldn't cope and she'd had enough. Finally, she confided that Harry's father had been sent to prison for fraud three weeks ago.

Discussion Points

For each case answer the following questions:

1. What emotional support does the child need?
2. What other help could the practitioner and/or setting offer?

Supporting children's emotional development involves developing an emotionally secure and safe environment for all children as a starting point. Young children need to be protected from bullying or negative behaviour from others and guided in developing assertiveness to cope with other more dominant children or adults.

Steps that can be taken to provide a positive environment for emotional development are:

♦ Create and maintain a secure, respectful and caring ethos between adults and children and between children through role modelling, agreeing standards, gentle reminders and discussion in circle time.

♦ Help children to develop skills to problem-solve emotional issues through tactful interventions, conversation, discussion in groups or using scenarios such as 'What ifs'?.

♦ Use the curriculum to support children's emotional development by helping them towards autonomous learning, gaining confidence in their own ability and by providing opportunities for self-expression.

♦ Keep stress levels down by maintaining a calm, orderly environment and giving extra support to children who are experiencing stress outside the setting.

♦ Support the development of self-esteem through opportunities for success, acknowledgement of achievement and emphasis on progress rather than development that has not taken place yet.

♦ Recognize that young children have strong emotions and feelings about many issues and that these need to be respected and not dismissed.

Social development is closely linked to emotional development. Young children's social behaviour in the setting may be determined by their experiences in the home and their emotional state, as well as the events immediately affecting them. As in any type of behaviour, role models at home and in the setting will have a strong influence on children's social behaviour. Children in the same group may have very different social experiences prior to coming into pre-school or school settings and this may influence their social behaviour significantly.

Supporting Positive Behavioural Development

Not all children have wide experience of other children or adults and some children may have been socially isolated by disability, family circumstances or cultural/ language differences. In any group there will be a wide range of social competency and it is important to recognize that expectations should not be based on the most competent children. Social competency is a developmental issue and children need to be supported and encouraged to make progress with this.

A key factor in social behavioural development is the quality of interactions between staff and children in the setting. Where practitioners are warm and responsive to children's individual needs, there are better outcomes for children in terms of social behaviour (*EPPE*, 2003). Practitioners also need to adopt strategies that both support children in being assertive but also involve talking through and making sense of conflicts (*EPPE*, 2003).

Certain children are more likely to struggle with social difficulties than others. These are:

◆ children with developmental delays or issues affecting cognitive development and social skills;

◆ children with emotional issues that affect behaviour e.g. withdrawn or aggressive behaviour that may isolate them socially;

◆ children who may be culturally different or have a different first language to other children in the group;

+ children with family issues that affect their stress levels and emotional stability.

Practitioners can support these children by:

+ role modelling positive behaviour towards socially isolated children;

+ keeping groups stable and promoting group support for children;

+ promoting social play, supporting isolated children in social play and providing opportunities for them to play in groups and pairs;
+ pairing the child with a more confident other or providing a support group who can help the child in play.

Meeting Social Needs

Cary, 4, is a large and loud child who has made his presence felt since joining the nursery class six months ago. The setting has tried to support and provide for his needs but Cary has been aggressive and physically intimidating with some of the younger children and has confronted staff on more than one occasion. Although Cary initially made friends among the older boys in the setting, they now avoid him, as he is disruptive in play and demands his own way at all times. When thwarted, Cary tends to destroy games and activities and shout or

---

hit other children. In outdoor play, Cary is usually very loud and active, but largely ignored by the other children. At the same time as dreading another outburst from Cary, the staff recognize that he is isolated and lonely and they are concerned that this will continue when he goes to school. They are concerned that Cary has difficulty concentrating, has poor skills in play and he seems unable to respond to others in a socially accepted way.

Discussion Points

1. What strategies might help Cary with his behaviour?
2. How could Cary be supported to develop more effective social skills?

In order to support social development, settings need to:

♦ ensure that children's social behaviour is monitored and tracked;

♦ specifically address social issues through the curriculum, circle time, discussions;

♦ ensure that social behaviour is discussed with parents and children;

♦ support children with social behavioural difficulties directly.

Developing Inclusive Settings

Drifte (2004) suggests that one of the reasons that we should develop inclusive settings is that strategies to support the behaviour of children with SEN will have a 'ripple' effect and benefit all children in the setting by extending good practice in care and education. She suggests the following ways of developing inclusive settings:

♦ all children work together;

♦ children with behavioural difficulties have specialist support if necessary;

♦ change practices, policies and attitudes to ensure the inclusion of all children;

♦ plan the curriculum to support the child's strengths and abilities;

♦ 'difference as ordinary' (p. 7);

♦ ensure the child's views are sought.

It is sometimes difficult to recognize when practices in the setting are not inclusive. Planning an inclusive curriculum is not just about differentiating activities to meet differing levels of ability; it is about doing different activities so all children can be involved.

Planning for Inclusion

Read the scenarios below and for each one write down what could have been done differently to support the child.

Ben, 6, is sitting colouring at a side desk while other children in the class are working on practice questions for their Year 2 SATs. Ben is not taking the SATs because he is statemented for complex needs, including significant delays in literacy and numeracy development.

Daisy, 3, is having a story read to her by the nursery nurse student while the other children are doing a topic on colour. Daisy is blind.

Tony, 5, is out in the playground with the teaching assistant, walking around. He has Asperger syndrome and has come out of the class because he is not managing to sit on the carpet for a story and he has become very fidgety and disruptive.

Jenny, 5, is sitting crying in the toilets of her new school. The topic is families and Jenny cannot remember her birth parents as she has been in care for two years. She does not know if she can call her new foster carers her family as she has only been with them for two weeks. Jenny is scared she will be asked questions about her family in front of the class.

Inclusion is not just about a set of practices to support children. It involves attitudinal change so that practitioners are thinking about inclusive practice in all their work with children, their planning and their behaviour management. If planning does not include consideration of different needs from the start, then children with SEN will continue to be excluded. There are some basic principles that need to be considered when working towards inclusion, but actual planning will depend on the needs of the children in a group and will vary according to these:

♦ Communicate with parents frequently and in-depth about their children's needs and how these can be met – parents are a rich source of information and can be supportive to the setting.

♦ Ask for information and support from other agencies when dealing with specific difficulties that you do not know much about.

♦ Plan together in the setting to maximize the child's inclusion in activities and play – do not plan and then think what you are going to do with the child with SEN!

♦ Learn about the child's behaviour through discussion and observation and try to avoid situations which you know will be too challenging for her.

♦ Talk to the child, within her capabilities, about what she likes to do, what is hard for her and what is not.

♦ Do not identify the child as different to the group, be

warm and supportive as with any child to promote her acceptance by the other children.

♦ Create a reliable group of mature children to support the child in group activities.

Management Strategies

The role of the manager in the setting, whether it be the headteacher, early years setting manager or children's centre manager, is crucial in determining behavioural standards and promoting this to the whole setting community. The manager has responsibility for determining the ethos and values that underpin behaviour management in the setting and for development of a behaviour management strategy. This is discussed in more detail in Chapter 5.

The manager's role includes:

♦ modelling positive behaviour with children, parents and staff;

♦ ensuring that there is a clearly stated vision or ethos about positive behaviour promotion in the setting and that this is supported by relevant policies (see Chapter 5);

♦ maintaining good standards of behaviour in the

setting through discussion, participation, training and support for others;

♦ supporting practitioners to promote positive behaviour through training and supervision;

♦ involving other agencies and outside support as required;

♦ supporting the participation of all members of the setting community in setting and maintaining behavioural standards;

♦ developing and maintaining an inclusive setting to support all children's needs.

Without a management-led vision of what behaviour is wanted and how behavioural development will be supported, practitioners will struggle to achieve progress in this area. The *EPPE* study showed that in less-effective settings there was a lack of coherence in the strategy to support behaviour as follows:

♦ no follow up on behavioural issues;

♦ behaviour is dealt with by simply telling children to stop;

♦ distraction is seen as a strategy for managing behaviour.

(EPPE, 2003)

Children need to have the opportunity to learn about their own behaviour and others' behaviour rather than incidents of difficult behaviour being responded to in isolation.

Staff training is a key element of behavioural development. Managers have a responsibility to ensure there is a comprehensive strategy for staff development in behaviour management to support the ethos of the setting. This needs to be underpinned by a good understanding of developmental issues for all children in the setting.

The Physical and Material Environment

The environment needs to be well planned and organized to provide children with a space for play and learning that suits their needs. A messy, disorganized environment can be frustrating and stressful for children and adults and may involve unnecessary disruptions to children's activities or lack of focus on these. Children with disabilities and/or SEN may find disorganized environments particularly stressful. Careful thought as to how space is used is also necessary for the practitioners to be able to oversee all of the activities within it. For example, one Foundation Stage 2 class had two adjoining rooms, one used for learning and one for play space.

Children often went into the play space in their own time after finishing planned activities, but it was difficult to manage both spaces at once and the play space quickly became disrupted with toys and equipment everywhere and children unable to find room to play within it. Key factors to consider when organizing the physical environment are:

♦ movement flows (can children and practitioners easily move around the space?);

♦ accessibility (can children and practitioners easily access materials, toys, equipment?);

♦ room for social play (can children play together and with practitioners in the spaces provided without being cramped?);

♦ quiet spaces away from more active play spaces;

♦ easy access to storage and simple procedures for packing away;

♦ flexibility so that spaces can be used for different purposes and adapted easily;

♦ a layout that allows practitioners an oversight of the children.

Establishing an Effective Physical Environment

The parent and child community playgroup has one paid organizer and relies on parent volunteers to ensure it works smoothly. It opens 10–12 every day. The organization of the volunteers is not very effective, meaning that it is often unclear who is doing what. The playgroup uses a community centre that is used by many other groups. Often it is left in a messy condition with tables and chairs piled around. The play materials and equipment for the playgroup are kept in a long, narrow cupboard and often it is easier to just get out the stuff nearest the door. Although activities are laid out with some plan in mind, this is rudimentary and unchanging. Care of the play materials and equipment is intermittent and much of it is in poor condition. The process of setting up seems to take up half the time the playgroup has in the centre and packing away is often done in a rush. The playgroup is well used and often very full. Children aged 0–4 use the group with their parents. Supervision of children is variable as parents use the group to meet their own social needs. The organizer is conscious that there is a high level of low-key friction between the children at times and that some children dominate the most popular activities and toys.

Discussion Points

1. What advice would you give the organizer?
2. Write out a plan of action to improve the children's experiences in this playgroup.

Partnership with Parents

Earlier in this chapter we looked at the role of parents in supporting the development of behavioural standards in a setting. Parental involvement needs to be central to any behaviour management strategy because:

♦ parents are children's main carers and the most influential adults in their lives;

♦ parenting approaches are central to the development of children's behaviour;

♦ parents have much experience of managing children's behaviour and will share this if encouraged to do so;

♦ collaboration is a key to good standards of behaviour management at home and in the setting;

♦ settings have a lot to offer parents who are struggling to support their children's behavioural development effectively;

♦ parental involvement with their children's learning and early years setting is a key factor in success for the child.

It is not difficult to see that working together on behavioural issues will also give the child a much clearer message about expectations than when this differs substantially between home and setting. However, involving all parents can be challenging, and sometimes it may feel that the parents you most want to involve are the hardest to reach. There are a number of reasons why parents may find it hard to get involved with the setting:

♦ they do not feel welcome or wanted in the setting;

♦ they do not feel they have anything to offer;

♦ they are concerned that you, the experts, the professionals, will be critical of them or not value their contributions;

♦ they may have had poor experiences of care and education in their own childhood and this may shape their views;

♦ they may be too busy with work and managing other aspects of their lives;

♦ they may not have the time or energy;

♦ they may have problems such as drug or alcohol dependency, mental or physical health issues, domestic violence or relationship breakdown which prevent them focusing on their child at present.

Supporting parents to become involved is not a single event. Settings need to have a coherent plan for encouraging parents to be involved and to feel comfortable contributing their own ideas and feelings. This plan could include:

♦ welcome strategies so parents always feel able to come into the setting;

♦ time to talk to the parent about their child or other issues;

♦ information boards, news-sheets and regular communications about the setting and the child;

♦ events for parents, requests for involvement and encouragement for parents to come and see what you do;

♦ an ethos that promotes respect for parents' views and opinions and recognizes their concerns and fears;

♦ plans for targeting parents who are less confident, who have English as a second language or who have learning difficulties;

♦ sympathetic and supportive advice available for parents who are in difficulties of any sort;

♦ specific support for parents who have children with SEN.

It is also important to remember that some parents may

use parenting approaches that you feel are unsupportive or even damaging to their child's development. This may create strong feelings among practitioners who see the outcome for the child, especially where there is abuse or neglect. Despite these feelings, creating and maintaining a relationship with parents, providing support and advice about behaviour management and role modelling effective strategies are still the best approaches. However, if you do recognize possible indicators of abuse or neglect in a child, your setting child protection procedures must be followed.

Getting a Wide Range of Parents Involved

In settings where parent partnership is flourishing, involving parents in behaviour management and behavioural development plans should not be a problem. However, a key factor in getting a range of parents involved is recognizing that for some parents the culture of the setting will feel more comfortable than for others.

Greenwood Primary

At a suburban primary school there seems to be a high level of parental involvement in both infants and nursery. Parent governor posts are easy to fill; there is a flourishing fund-raising body; school trips always have enough volunteers; parents come into school to support reading development in infants and to share their skills in cooking, sewing, gardening and sport. Closer analysis

---

shows that in fact there is quite a small number of parents actually involved and these are almost all white middle-class women. Although the school has a substantial number of children from British Asian families and less well-off families, parents from these groups are largely not involved. Very few men are involved with the school's activities.

Discussion Points

1. Give some reasons why some parents are less likely to be involved in the school.
2. Write a plan for involving a more varied range of parents of infant and nursery children in the school's management and activities.

Partnership with Other Professionals and Agencies

The development of multi-disciplinary settings has demonstrated that, for many children and their families, support is best provided through a multi-disciplinary approach, drawing on the expertise of different professionals to ensure that support is effective and timely. Sure Start local programmes, and now children's centres, provide a range of services to some children and their families in areas of disadvantage, and within these practitioners are able to draw on each other's expertise as required. Within schools, children with special educational needs can be supported through School Action Plus, involving agencies such as social services, CAMHS, health services and family support agencies to ensure that the child's needs are met in a coherent well-planned way. Statemented children receive assessment and support from a similar range of agencies. Recent policy

♦ other agencies/professionals providing direct services to the child and/or family.

Seeking Support from Other Agencies

Look at the example of Adam on page 103.

1. What other types of support could CAMHS offer the school or the child?
2. What other sources of support could be sought and from which agency/professional?

Consider the links you have with other professionals/ agencies in your setting.

1. How do these support your setting with behaviour management issues?
2. What other support could they provide?
3. What other agencies/professionals could provide additional support for behaviour management in your setting and in what areas e.g. individual children, policy development, training and staff development?

When seeking support from other professionals/ agencies about a specific child, confidentiality issues need to be considered and permission for information sharing sought from parents. However, the *Children Act, 2004* has established the legal basis for electronic information sharing between key agencies and this may allow for more information to be shared more easily, although confidentiality requirements will still apply.

Developing Communication Strategies

A key aspect to developing partnership with parents and other agencies/professionals and consistent approaches to behaviour management within the setting is effective communication. Developing good communication strategies is often left to chance and this sometimes works to some extent, but not always, and not in all areas where communication is required.

Communication within the setting:

The following points could be a starting point for thinking about whether communication strategies within the setting are effective in supporting behavioural development and behaviour management:

♦ How are the principles and ethos of behaviour management in the setting developed and disseminated?

♦ How is the behaviour management policy developed and who is involved?

♦ How is the policy disseminated to all parents, practitioners and other adults involved with the setting?

Managing Behaviour in the Early Years

♦ How is the behaviour management policy explained to children?

♦ How do children know what is expected of them?

♦ What discussions take place about supporting children's emotional and social development through the curriculum?

♦ How are behavioural issues dealt with in teams hin the setting to ensure consistency of approach?

ιunication outside the setting:

at arrangements does the setting have for com-nicating with parents about behavioural issues?

be part of this ongoing discussion and have access to advice and support about dealing with behaviour and supporting children's behavioural development.

Learning the Rules

Dan, 4, has just started Reception class in a primary school. He knows the school well as his sisters attend, but he went to a different nursery where he developed a strong sense of his own value to the setting and where his self-esteem was good. The nursery staff had experience and skills in meeting Dan's special needs, which include global developmental delays, and he was an integrated and well-thought-of part of the nursery community. Dan looked forward to going to school and being part of a wider community meeting new children

> **Discussion Points**
>
> 1. What communication strategies could be used to introduce children to expectations within a new setting?
> 2. What do children need to know about these expectations?

Summary and Conclusions

In this chapter some of the strategies that can be used to develop positive behaviour have been discussed including partnership, communication, whole-setting approaches and the behaviour of practitioners and managers. Some of the ways in which aspects of children's development can be supported to promote behavioural development have been discussed and ways of including children with SEN outlined. The key message is that in order to achieve positive behaviour, all aspects of the setting must be considered in terms of the needs of all children. Knowledge and understanding of the child's needs are central to success and practitioners should be communicating with parents, other professionals/agencies and each other in order to ensure that they have sufficient knowledge to support the child's holistic development.

Policy development should involve discussion and debate, information searches, reading, thinking, arguing and negotiating. Writing down the policy should be the end product of a creative, fruitful process that determines ways of working, common standards and approaches and which strengthens and promotes the ethos and underpinning values in the setting.

In this chapter, the role and functions of behaviour management policies are discussed. The process of policy development will be outlined along with the value of sharing this process with partners and children. Policy development as a dynamic, ongoing process is a key theme along with a discussion about the underpinning values and principles within policy development. Dissemination of policies and their role in developing a common ethos and approach among staff is also discussed. Finally, the importance of monitoring and reviewing policies and evaluating their impact on practice is covered.

What are Policies For?

Putting aside inspection requirements for the moment, policies are everywhere in an early years setting. They guide what staff, children and parents do and how they do it. They determine what happens if there is a problem or if something goes wrong. They ensure consistency, determine behaviour and provide a framework for decision-making. Not all policies are written down, but many of the main areas of activity in an early years setting are the subject of a written policy. Sometimes there is a contradiction between written policy and what actually happens, because the 'real' policy is unwritten custom and practice.

Some policies are required by the LEA or Ofsted, while others are seen as good practice. Attitudes to policies vary. Some staff regard policy documents as working tools to guide behaviour and determine decision-making. Others follow policy, but not from written documents.

So, what are policies for?

♦ to make a statement about aims and objectives;

♦ to outline underpinning values and principles;

♦ to standardize practice and behaviour;

♦ to create a common understanding of key issues in the setting and with parents, children and others;

♦ to create a vision of good practice and how this can be achieved;

♦ to fulfil regulatory requirements;

♦ to monitor and evaluate practice and make improvements.

♦ practices and procedures to operationalize these plans;

♦ allocation of roles and responsibilities within procedures and practices;

♦ guidance for how to resolve issues or problems if they arise;

♦ monitoring and review arrangements for the policy.

Policy development requires scrutiny of your own practice and the principles underpinning this and a chance to discuss different approaches. This is not always easy to achieve and may be difficult, especially for new practitioners who hesitate to challenge the perceived wisdom. Managers need to be aware of this and to provide a forum where open debate is encouraged and supported.

The Process of Developing Behaviour Management Policies

Developing policies that effectively reflect the setting's approach to behaviour management takes time. Rogers (2000: 207) describes the process as a 'journey of change' from 'here' to 'there'. 'Here' is current thinking and practice around behaviour management. 'There' is the desired direction for progress in developing

150

1. Why does the policy need developing?
This may be because the setting is new and there is no policy as yet, or it is due for a review or that an inspection is due. It may be that a general 'spring clean' of policies is going on.

2. Who should be involved?
The best answer to this is, as Drifte (2004: 27) says, 'everybody appropriately involved in the setting'. This should include practitioners and other members of staff; parents; children; and professionals from other agencies who are involved with the setting. However, Rogers (2000) points out that the degree of consultation that actually takes place depends on the willingness of the setting to make the effort. Involving others is time consuming and may result in a mass of contradictory opinions and viewpoints. However, the benefits of a wide consultation are overwhelming. Involvement in developing a policy gives each individual a stake in the outcomes of that process, a deep understanding of the content and meaning of the policy and an investment in abiding by the provisions of the policy and taking their roles and responsibilities seriously.

3. How can we involve parents?
Involving parents can be through formal and informal meetings, questionnaires, asking parents to be on the policy writing team or asking them their views in the

corridor, as they pick the children up or drop them off. Parents' responses may vary, but most will value being asked and one of the positive side effects of this can be a feeling of being more involved in the setting. Another side effect of consulting parents and getting them involved in the debate about best practice in behaviour management is a clearer understanding of what sort of behaviour management strategies are used in the home. Parents may modify their approaches in the light of this sharing of views and the setting may modify theirs. There is a lot to learn from each other. Having a stake in the policy may encourage parents to use similar methods in the home and the child will benefit from the increased consistency this leads to. It is important to be open about potentially involving all parents and not just 'cherry picking' those most likely to agree with what you do already.

4. How can we involve children?
Children may have a lot to say about how they would like to relate to each other and the adults around them. There are many ways of getting to know their views on behaviour, and the strategy used will depend on the age of the children and what you know of what works for them. Some ideas are to ask the children what rules they should have to help everyone to get on well together, or ask them what sort of ways they can be kind to each other. It is important to explain to the children in terms

similar policies; visits to other settings; relevant staff development courses).

♦ The principles underpinning the policy. (What are our values? What ethos do we want to create in the setting?)

♦ What advice do we get from the LEA (or other professional bodies such as National Day Nurseries Association, National Childminding Association)?

Although it is useful to look at policies from other settings or sample policies that can be found on the Internet, it is the process of policy-making that creates the common understanding and ethos and embeds the principles of behaviour management across the setting. Using a ready-made policy does not take the setting through this process and therefore has little value.

The working party then has responsibility for drafting the policy and circulating it for comment. The policy could include:

♦ a statement about the purposes of the policy;

♦ a statement of beliefs;

♦ a statement of aims and objectives;

♦ how these are to be achieved;

♦ the responsibilities of different individuals within the policy (practitioners, managers, children);

This approach gives the children and adults guidelines on what behaviour is expected and seen as positive.

Once drafts have been completed they should be circulated for comment and revised accordingly before publication.

8. How long should the policy be?
Some policies are so long that it can be said with absolute truth that no one has ever waded through them since they were written and therefore they are useless as working documents to support positive practice. The balance to find here is between a very long policy that no one will use and one that is short and has impact but does not include key information.

Edgington (1998) points out that we sometimes mistake policy for guidelines, which are much more detailed and lengthy. She argues that policies are public documents and guidelines are to support the work of the team. It may be that the approach chosen by the setting is to have both a short and an extended version of the policy. Short versions may be produced for parents and for children so that policy can be presented in a simple and readable form. However, these short versions may not be sufficient to guide practitioners in their work with children and should be supported by an extended version.

9. What do we do with the policy now?
Hopefully not put it on a shelf with the other policies and watch it gather dust! The policy should be disseminated in some form to parents, made available to children in the setting and given out to practitioners, or at least made easily available to them. A children's version can be made into a poster with simple statements which can be displayed around the setting. Copies of the written policy should be available throughout the setting and there should be a mechanism for new staff and students to be made aware of the location of all policies in the setting.

10. Is that it?
The last thing that settings need to do is to go through the hard work of developing behaviour management policies and then not using the final product to inform practice. Keeping the debate about an issue such as behaviour management alive is both important and very difficult at times. However, a policy that is the product of wide consultation and debate is more likely to maintain behaviour management as a live issue than one produced by a small number of people behind closed doors. Policy development takes place in the process not the product and hopefully at the end of this process the ethos and practice of behaviour management in the setting will be widely understood by practitioners, parents, children and relevant others. However it is important to:

are being met. This process is often the forgotten part of policy development and in some cases progress towards achieving policy aims may not be considered until the policy is reviewed. Edgington (1998) suggests the following ways of evaluating practice against policy aims:

♦ gathering evidence to show if the policy is being translated into practice e.g. through observation;

♦ evaluating aspects of the policy through discussion in team meetings;

♦ asking parents and governors for feedback on the extent to which policy aims are being achieved in practice.

It may be useful to use the behaviour management policy with children as a basis for discussion about behaviour in their group and whether this has been positive. This can be a way of giving positive feedback to children about their behaviour.

Summary and Conclusions

In this chapter, the process and practice of writing behaviour management policies have been discussed and the value of this process to the setting outlined in terms of:

6 Managing Individual Behaviour

The reason this significant chapter comes last in the book is because it is hoped that managing individual behaviour will take place in the context of your understanding of influences on children's behaviour (including individual children's developmental issues); a whole setting approach to creating a positive environment for behavioural development; and the development of a dynamic, relevant and well-established behaviour policy. Managing individual behaviour does not take place in isolation from the rest of the activities and events in the setting or outside the ethos and principles determining how that setting operates. Consideration of some of the issues discussed above and practical application of strategies to provide a supportive, sensitive environment in which children can learn and develop confidently may well reduce the number and intensity of incidents of individual behaviour that need managing. However, as

Managing Behaviour in the Early Years

Types of behaviour that may be the result of inexperience are:

♦ over-exuberance for the situation or circumstances;

♦ lack of respect or consideration for others;

♦ sulky, withdrawn, uncooperative behaviour;

♦ tantrums (if the child cannot get what he wants);

♦ tears and distress;

♦ shouting, angry expression, swearing;

♦ physical aggression, such as hitting, kicking, biting, throwing things at others;

♦ destruction or damage to materials.

Learning Patience

We often expect young children to have extraordinary patience in such things as waiting for their turn, waiting for adults or waiting for help, and yet they may simply not have developed to the stage where patience is part of their abilities.

Dan is nearly 3 but has some developmental delays. He is small for his age and emotionally immature. He has poor concentration and is very physically active. Dan loves the pre-school he attends because they have a red and yellow plastic pedal car. He does not have anything

---

a more fundamental basis than the more day-to-day ups and downs discussed above.

Young children become disaffected when they feel alienated from the process of learning and the activities of the setting. This may be because they feel devalued and incompetent within the setting. Children need to feel competent to learn in the setting or they become 'confused and frustrated, and disillusionment sets in'. (Fisher, 2002: 135). A key factor is whether the child's expectations are in line with the setting's expectations.

Children may feel alienated for many different reasons, some of which are discussed in Chapter 2 and relate to family and social circumstances. For other children these feelings may come from feeling 'different' to other children, possibly because of developmental issues or because they are from a cultural or social background that is less compatible with that of the setting. Other reasons are that the expectations of the child in the setting may be out of step with her developmental stage (and this can apply to gifted children as well as children with learning delays). For some children this may mean that the ways of learning asked of them are not what they expect, in the sense that the child may have learned differently prior to coming into the setting, or the ways of learning do not draw on the child's strengths. For example, a child with dyslexia may constantly feel frustrated at his inability to keep up with other children in literacy development. He may have strong oral skills but if these are not valued as much as the reading and writing he finds so difficult he may easily become disillusioned. A child who feels that he cannot meet the demands made of him in the setting or that what he has to offer is not of value in the setting may simply opt out.

The author used to work with excluded school pupils aged 14 and 15 in a college setting, where they were provided with vocational education as an alternative to school. The students were almost all boys and most had demonstrated behaviours extreme enough to earn them permanent exclusions from more than one school. Gradually through conversation and observation the author learned that most of these boys had these features in common:

♦ they were all summer born;
♦ all of them had suffered family breakdown or disruption;
♦ about 50 per cent lived in a single-parent father-headed family;
♦ they had all left primary school with significant delays in their literacy development;
♦ their behavioural problems had become significant in Year 8 and their exclusions had started in Year 9;
♦ they had all learned that angry, aggressive or extreme behaviour would remove them from learning situations in which they felt incapable of success;

Dealing with Confused Feelings and Low Self-Esteem

Laila, 6, has just started her third school in two years. Her mother has moved twice in order to escape domestic violence from her partner, Laila's father. Laila has no significant developmental issues but her learning has been delayed due to poor early experience and lack of consistency in her care. The moves have taken their toll on her confidence in school and she is withdrawn and uncooperative with her teacher and other children, so she is often isolated inside and outside the classroom. Laila is very confused and angry about the events that have taken place in her home. She is angry with both parents and sad that she has not seen her father for some time, although she is very scared of him. Laila has started to pinch other children in the class, especially those who sit on her table. She does not seem to do this in response to anything the other child does, but the behaviour seems designed to disrupt learning and cause upset among the other children.

Discussion Points

1. What do you need to know about Laila to help her?
2. What sort of response would be effective in this situation?

unwanted behaviour from that child. The sorts of things that are useful to know about a child are:

- the child's character and personality;
- the circumstances and location;
- the time of day and the learning context;
- the reasons for the child's behaviour;
- the group the child is in and who else is involved;
- whether the behaviour is part of a pattern or not;
- what the behaviour is and the severity of the behaviour;
- whether the behaviour is a risk to the child, other children, adults or property.

Developing a Range of Responses

Practitioners need to develop a range of responses and expertise in using these in the right situations. There is always going to be a certain amount of trial and error about this and practitioners need to be clear that changing approaches that are not working is a positive step. Sticking to your first approach because you do not want to be seen to 'back down' is pointless if that approach is ineffectual. There are a number of ways practitioners can develop a range of different approaches and knowledge of when to use them:

- ◆ observing and talking to more experienced practitioners;

- ◆ talking to parents;

- ◆ accessing relevant training;

- ◆ reading;

- ◆ practising;

- ◆ reviewing the effectiveness of approaches after the event;

- ◆ developing a personal approach and philosophy.

Not all approaches suit everyone. It is important to find ways of responding to children's unwanted behaviour that are effective but that fit in with your own philosophy and style and the policy and ethos of the setting.

Underpinning Principles

Any response to a child's behaviour needs to be based on a philosophy and principles about what you are trying to achieve and how you are trying to achieve it. In this book, a developmental approach to managing behaviour has been suggested and the principles listed below are based on this. In your setting or your own

+ the child is expressing herself and is engaged and involved in activities or play;

+ the child does not regularly behave in disruptive ways and this is not a pattern of behaviour.

It is important to continue to observe the child so that if the behaviour changes or the situation changes another response can be introduced as necessary.

> Jake, 3, is singing loudly and in an off-key tone during outdoor play. At times he is almost howling. The other children are joining in at times and laughing at Jake's horrible sounds. Jake is enjoying the attention and having fun. As no one is getting hurt or upset, you resist the urge to put a stop to the noise and after a few minutes the children move on to another game and Jake stops.

Remind the child of the rules/boundaries/expectations:

The child may simply have forgotten that it is not acceptable to run in the corridor or throw toys at the storage boxes before moving on to something else. Children can become very absorbed in their play and activities and following the rules can be a hindrance to the flow of their learning sometimes. Reminding a child of what is expected can be effective if this is the reason for the behaviour. However, Porter (2003) points out that repeated reminders are pointless as the child

children are particularly sensitive about 'getting things wrong' and will need a lot of reassurance. Tone of voice is very important in this type of interaction. Avoid 'told you so' tones or instruction and discuss the issues in a matter-of-fact tone.

Fazan, 5, is doing a jigsaw puzzle. He has found it very hard to match the pieces to the gaps and has needed a lot of help. While you are responding to another child, he jams a piece in the wrong place and then when he cannot get it back out he throws the jigsaw across the table and shouts a rude word. You go over to Fazan and tell him you will help him pick up the jigsaw. When the pieces are back on the table you sit and do it with him, giving him the clues for working out which pieces go where.

Help the child with things she is struggling with:

One of the main complaints I have heard so many times from my own children through their time in school and nursery is that they have not had help when they needed it or even when they have asked for it. Leaving children to struggle is very different to leaving them to work things out for themselves. It does not teach them autonomy or help them to work more independently. It merely frustrates and distresses them. Often children only need a little help to know they are on the right track or to get started. Some children have much less confidence than others in working independently, and building confidence takes time and support.

> Dan, 2, is trying to put a shape in a shape sorter. He is dyspraxic and he finds it difficult to manipulate the piece into the hole although he has matched these successfully. He is getting very angry and beating the shape on the floor. You take his hand and gently turn it so the piece goes into the slot. You do the same when he struggles with the next piece.

Stop sequences of behaviour at an early stage:

How many times have we all heard the phrase 'If you do that again, I'll . . .'? To many children this is a positive invitation to do 'that' again just to see what happens next. In some situations children are threatened repeatedly with consequences to their behaviour which are then not forthcoming, or when they come belatedly are disproportionate because the adult has lost her temper. If your knowledge of a child tells you that a disruptive sequence of behaviour has commenced, then you know to stop it before it gets under way. Change the situation, remove the child by encouraging him towards another area, remove the focus of attention from the child. One useful approach is to sit or stand near the child calmly discussing other issues. Above all, do not give the child a chance to challenge you with the behaviour.

- Tell the child what you want him to do rather than tell him what he should not be doing (he may already know that he should not be doing it).

- Explain to the child what the consequences of her behaviour may be and why she should not behave in this way, but do not use these explanations to go on at a child at length.

- Acknowledge that controlling emotions can be hard for the child.

- Be problem-solving: 'How can we sort this out?' and use this as a way of calming the child: 'If you calm down we can sort this out.'

- Respond to the distress children may have at losing control by providing comfort and warmth.

- Let a distressed child have time to calm down and some time alone if needed.

Practitioners also need to ensure that there is no physical or other cause for the behaviour. You may need to check the following:

- Is the child unwell?

- Is the child hungry?

- Has something happened to distress the child prior to the behaviour?

- he comes to be seen in a negative light;

- children and practitioners may not feel or behave warmly to him;

- he becomes a problem to 'solve';

- he may become socially isolated;

- his time in the setting is judged in terms of his behaviour only.

It is easy sometimes to get into patterns of thinking about a child that are anxious and negative and to become hopeless about helping children with chronic behaviour problems. It is important to try to break out of these and spend time thinking of alternative approaches.

Prevention:

Chapter 5 outlines many of the strategies that can be used to create a positive environment for behavioural development on a setting-wide basis.

In terms of individual children other preventative strategies to consider are:

- Has the child been recognized as having SEN and has she got an Individual Education Plan (IEP)?

- What sort of support from other agencies and professionals is needed and has this been secured?

- Is there a positive cooperative relationship with parents and, if not, how can this be developed?

- Are the issues for the child fully understood and, if not, what further assessment would you suggest?

Developing Strategies:

- these should be the result of teamwork with other practitioners, other professionals and parents;

- if a strategy is not working, avoid the tendency to blame the child and then change the strategy;

- be sure that the chosen strategy addresses the child's issues and that these are fully understood;

- try to consider support strategies that will help the child move on, not those that just contain his behaviour;

- take time out to think about the child, discuss him with others, read around similar behavioural issues and try to get a fresh view of his issues;

- break up patterns of behaviour by responding differently and giving the child a chance to change;

- signal to managers and your support network if you are becoming exhausted and fatalistic about the child's behaviour;

behaviour management policies developed and 'owned' by the whole setting community.

Dealing with individual behavioural issues needs to be in the context of this wider whole-setting approach in order to create environments in which most children's behavioural development will flourish. In order to achieve successful behavioural development for individual children, practitioners need information and knowledge about the children in their care and about developmental issues that may affect children's behaviour. They need a range of strategies and the knowledge and ability to match their approach to the child's needs and to develop the approach if the child is not responding.

Behaviour management is not a single event focused on an individual child's behaviour. It is a complex range of interrelated approaches that both create better environments for behavioural development and support children where this development requires additional help.

References

Action for Autistic Spectrum Disorders http://www.actionasd.org.uk last accessed on 14/3/05.

Baumrind, D. (1967) *Child care practices anteceding three patterns of pre-school behaviour*, Genetic Psychology Monographs 75, pp. 43–88.

Baumrind, D. (1973) 'The development of instrumental competence through socialization' in Pick, A.E. (ed.) *Minnesota symposium on child psychology*, Minneapolis: University of Minnesota Press, pp. 3–46.

Bee, H. (2000) *The Developing Child* (9th ed.), Needham Heights, MA: Allyn and Bacon.

Belsky, J. (1984) *The Determinants of Parenting: a Process Model*, Child Development, 55, pp. 83–96.

Belsky, J. and Vondra, J. (1989) 'Lessons from Child Abuse: The Determinants of Parenting', in Cicchetti, D. and Carlson, V. (eds) *Child Maltreatment*, Cambridge: Cambridge University Press.

References

Kay, J. (2003b) *Teacher's Guide to Protecting Children*, London: Continuum.

Maccoby, E.E. and Martin, J.A. (1983) 'Socialization in the context of the family' in Hetherington, E.M. (ed.) *Handbook of Child Psychology: vol. 4: Personality and social development* (4th ed.), New York: Wiley, pp. 1–101.

Moffit, T.E. (1993) *The neuropsychology of conduct disorder*, Development and Psychopathology 5(2), pp. 135–52.

Ofsted (March 2005) *Managing Challenging Behaviour* http://www.Ofsted.gov.uk/publication/index.cfm?fuseaction=publications.displayfile&id=3846&type=pdf last accessed 6/5/05.

Pierce, E., Ewing, L. and Campbell, S. (1999) *Diagnostic status and symptomatic behaviour of hard-to-manage preschool children in middle childhood and early adolescence*, Journal of Clinical Child Psychology 28 (10), pp. 44–57.

Porter, L. (2003) *Young Children's Behaviour: practical approaches for caregivers and teachers* (2nd ed.), London: Paul Chapman.

QCA (2000) *Curriculum Guidance for the Foundation Stage.*

Roffey, S. (2004) *The New Teacher's Survival Guide to Behaviour*, London: Paul Chapman.

Rogers, B. (2000) *Behaviour Management – A Whole School Approach*, London: Paul Chapman.

Lightning Source UK Ltd.
Milton Keynes UK
UKOW07f0502211114

241959UK00012B/180/P